Praise for *Coming of Age at the En...*

"Though they did little to create the planetary pickle we're
in, these young writers and thinkers embody the optimism,
determination, and courage we'll need to get out of it."

—**Chip Giller**, founder of *Grist*

"Ignore this book at your peril! *Coming of Age at the End of Nature*
is a stunning collection from young writers who have grown
up with environmental crisis and the disruption and danger
of climate change. These powerful new voices disturb our
traditional notions of wilderness and wandering through
sylvan scenes. In a world of suburban sprawl, urban blight, and
glittering neon consumerism, they redefine how we look at
nature and ourselves."

—**Robert Musil**, president of the Rachel Carson Council
and author of *Washington in Spring: A Nature Journal for a
Changing Capital*

"*Coming of Age at the End of Nature* is a gift of sanity and a revelation
of wisdom. The resourcefulness filling these pages reclaims
the root of the word meaning 'to rise again, recover.' By
answering for their lives with deep maturity, responsibility, and
adaptability, these young writers ask us as readers to answer for
our own. You will not find elegies here but clear, provocative
insights that reveal the circumstances and contexts in which we
all exist in relation to each other and the world we inhabit. It is
a privilege to read and learn from this wonderful book, which
calls on me to hold to what is difficult and necessary as well as
beautiful."

—**Lauret Savoy**, author of *Trace: Memory, History, Race, and the
American Landscape*

"*Coming of Age at the End of Nature* is an important book. Not important because it contains a set of beautifully imagined and deeply thoughtful and lovingly written essays—though it does. Not important because we, all of us, live in a time of great and uneasy change, and we badly need beautifully imagined, deeply thoughtful, and lovingly written essays in the same way we need clean air and water, meaningful climate legislation, and bold leadership—though we do. It is an important book because it embodies the experiences, dreams, thoughts, fears, righteous anger, joy, and ultimately the audacious moral fiber of the generation now coming of age in the dangerous and degraded world, a world that we created and they now inherit."

> —**Michael Nelson**, coeditor of *Moral Ground: Ethical Action for a Planet in Peril*

"*Coming of Age at the End of Nature* is a must-read for anyone who's interested in engaging the next generation of conversation leadership. And we all should be very interested in engaging the next generation of conservation leadership. Relevancy is a critical issue for this movement. This book is a window into how young people think about and connect to the environment in their daily lives."

> —**Sarah Milligan-Toffler**, executive director of the Children and Nature Network

Coming of Age
at the End of Nature

Coming of Age at the End of Nature

*A Generation Faces Living
on a Changed Planet*

Edited by

Julie Dunlap & Susan A. Cohen

FOREWORD BY BILL McKIBBEN

Trinity University Press
San Antonio

Published by Trinity University Press
San Antonio, Texas 78212

Copyright © 2016 by Julie Dunlap and Susan A. Cohen

All rights reserved. No part of this book may be reproduced in any form or
by any electronic or mechanical means, including information storage and
retrieval systems, without permission in writing from the publisher.

Cover illustration and design by Sarah Cooper
Book design by BookMatters

ISBN-13 978-1-59534-780-0 paper
ISBN-13 978-1-59534-778-7 ebook

Trinity University Press strives to produce its books using methods and
materials in an environmentally sensitive manner. We favor working with
manufacturers that practice sustainable management of all natural resources,
produce paper using recycled stock, and manage forests with the best
possible practices for people, biodiversity, and sustainability. The press is
a member of the Green Press Initiative, a nonprofit program dedicated to
supporting publishers in their efforts to reduce their impacts on endangered
forests, climate change, and forest-dependent communities.

The paper used in this publication meets the minimum requirements of the
American National Standard for Information Sciences—Permanence of
Paper for Printed Library Materials, ANSI 39.48–1992.

CIP data on file at the Library of Congress

20   19   18   17   16   5   4   3   2   1

Contents

II. THINKING LIKE A RIVER

III. MINDFUL MONKEYWRENCHING

Foreword

BILL McKIBBEN

To say that this book is a particular delight for me would be an understatement. I wrote *The End of Nature* when I was twenty-seven, and when I go back to read it now some parts seem jejune. That's not true of the writing in *Coming of Age at the End of Nature*, which is mature, reflective, deep, and lovely. It makes me hopeful.

Which is, of course, a certain irony, because in the intervening three decades much has happened to relieve us of hope, as many of these commentators make clear. What was an abstract fear of climate change in the late 1980s is, by the middle 2010s, a crisis so deep it's possible to argue that we've simply waited too long to get started. I don't quite believe that, which is why I spend my life as one in a great army of activists—a movement ably limned in these pages. There are people in this book I've linked arms with in nonviolent protests or worked with on crucial projects; there are, happily, many more I've encountered only through their words—proof of how big and broad the new environmentalism is.

I've been consciously backing off from formal leadership in that movement for some years now, mostly to open the way for young people who will be fighting this fight until they're my age or beyond. The passion and insight in these pages give me hope, as always, that the fight will keep growing, encompassing more and different kinds of people, finding new openings to the hearts and souls of our fellow human beings.

But I'm also heartened by the sheer, dogged commitment to observing the world in all its beauty, even as that beauty is compromised. The planet we were given will never be more intact or whole than it is at this moment, and one of our jobs as human beings (and surely as writers) is simply to bear witness to it in all its glory, mystery, buzzing cruelty.

I am so grateful to the writers in this book and to the thought that I am part of their company of observers, thinkers, doers. The world is in a tough place, but it doesn't lack for witnesses and partisans!

Introduction

How has growing up in a mutable physical, biological, and social world shaped the lives and thoughts of today's young adults? What do members of this generation have to say about their challenges, hopes, fears, and sources of resilience for the unpredictable future? Shrinking Arctic ice caps and healing ozone holes, dwindling biodiversity and expanding environmental education, ocean acidification and advancing global monitoring technology, and intransigent climate change denial amid burgeoning climate activism have been formative realities in their early lives. The essays collected here are composed by a particular set of insightful young adults: talented writers belonging to a generation that grew to maturity inundated with news and personal experiences of unprecedented environmental change. Together, they attempt to answer what it means—to them—to come of age in a time of shifting expectations and environmental crisis.

Humans have shaped the natural world deliberately and incidentally for millennia, but previous generations perceived environmental problems as primarily local—clearing of a forest, draining of a wetland, extirpation of a game fish—and retained confidence that human damage would heal over time through nature's resilience. But by the late twentieth century, traces of human influence reached everywhere, from heavy metal pollution in undersea sediments to CFCs in the stratosphere. In 1989, before many of our contributors were born, Bill McKibben wrote in *The End of Nature* that human influence on the planet has grown ubiquitous; pristine wilderness no longer exists. To McKibben, contamination of the upper atmosphere with anthropogenic greenhouse gases is the ultimate sign of nature's end, or at least the end of humanity's ancient relationship with the natural world: "We have not ended rainfall or sunlight; in fact, rainfall and sunlight may become more important forces in our lives. . . . But the 'meaning' of the wind, the sun, the rain—of nature—has already changed." *Coming of Age at the End of Nature* attempts to reveal how this change in fundamental relationships has influenced the first generation to grapple throughout their lives with these altered realities.

Today's young-adult generation—a vast group born between about 1980 and 2000—has been closely scrutinized to understand its demographics, influences, attitudes, and behaviors. Several studies, such as the Pew Research Center's 2010 "Millennials: A Portrait of Generation Next," describe the age cohort as more ethnically diverse, more educated, and less economically secure than their elders. Comparative research, however, has not determined that millennials are consistently "greener" than Baby Boomers or members of Generation X. "The Climate Change Generation?

Survey Analysis of the Perceptions and Beliefs of Young Americans," a major 2010 study by American University, Yale University, and George Mason University, focused specifically on climate change views of young adults, noting that "American adults under the age of 35 have come of age in the decades since the 'discovery' of man-made climate change as a major social problem." That national survey revealed that young adults have complex attitudes toward global warming, with some striking contrasts with older generations. As examples, young adults are more likely than their elders to recognize the scientific consensus about climate change and to believe that damage will occur in the relatively near future (ten to fifty years). But only 38 percent of eighteen- to thirty-four-year-olds said they thought about climate change "some" or "a lot," compared with 51 percent of adults aged thirty-five to fifty-nine.

The diversity of millennials further complicates sociological analysis of their viewpoints. The joint university study, looking at age groups within the greater cohort, found the college-aged subgroup viewed climate change consequences as imminent more often than older subgroups, and perceived more climate change–related activity among their friends; 10 percent of eighteen- to twenty-two-year-olds strongly agreed that their friends were acting to reduce warming, compared with just 3 percent of twenty-three- to thirty-four-year-olds. Millennials of all ages who identified as conservatives were more skeptical and less engaged on climate issues than liberals in the study, but large majorities of generation members of all political ideologies trusted scientists as sources of climate information (100 percent of liberals, 84 percent of moderates, 68 percent of conservatives). "Overall," the researchers conclude, the study provides "no predictable portrait of young people when it comes to global warming." The complex and often surprising survey results make listening to millennials' individual viewpoints still more imperative.

Thus far, a few millennial activist voices have emerged to speak for their age peers. Harvard Divinity School student Tim DeChristopher, for example, conveys his value-driven opposition to fossil fuels from microphones on courthouse steps, at invited conference speeches, on *Late Night with David Letterman*, and in the film *Bidder 70*. We sought, in calling for essays for this book, to engage a broader range of youthful perspectives, including activists but also teachers, editors, journalists, ecologists, community organizers, urban farmers, novelists, cooks, and poets. The wealth of submissions was winnowed carefully, to craft a selection by writers from a range of geographic and economic backgrounds and ethnic and cultural heritage. The full spectrum of millennial generation ages is represented: some are college students, others are exploring graduate school or first jobs, and others are established in professions and even parents (or prospective parents) themselves. A few of the pieces have appeared elsewhere, and several of the writers have published other work in *Orion*, *Sage Magazine*, and other journals. But one of this anthology's strengths, we believe, is the predominance of emerging voices, whose first appearance in print will be a consideration of their place in a world at a turning point.

Perhaps not surprisingly, few of the pieces focus on traditional, observational nature writing. Rather, across a range of styles and topics, the contributors explore human relationships to often damaged landscapes and waterways, wildlands and urban spaces, and to the permeable borders between them. Even when a writer delves into the intimate details of a beloved place, a tone of threat and loss inevitably resonates. Redeeming notes of hope in the face of challenges may, or may not, harmonize along. These creative writers, while enmeshed in the context of climate change, explore a rich variety of often overlapping themes. Materialism, shrinking biodiversity, rebounding wildness in urbanized landscapes, technological optimism, and the hubris of past generations are just a few.

As we read and reread our final selections, their basic themes cohered around three thought-provoking ideas.

Disheartened by evidence of irreversible anthropogenic environmental damage, Bill McKibben argues in *Eaarth: Making a Life on a Tough New Planet* (2010) that alterations to the planet are so significant that it deserves a modified name: Eaarth. Seismic shifts in understanding our place in the cosmos dominate the reflections and observations in the first group of essays. Anger rises in several selections, as writers rail against the human-sullied ecosystems they were born to depend upon. In the first part of the anthology, "Living on Eaarth," Ben Goldfarb mourns lost opportunities, asking how to choose a home place when each possibility now seems fragile and transient. But as reflected in Amaris Ketcham's "Urban Foraging," these writers are also determined to survive—even thrive—on Planet Eaarth. Despite hardships past and future, Ketcham vows to find ways to adapt because "we're still the same basic creatures we've been for millions of years."

The second part of the book, "Thinking like a River," speaks to pioneering ecologist Aldo Leopold's metaphor for "thinking like a mountain" to encourage long-term, holistic ecosystem conservation. The metaphor accepts environmental alterations that evolve through geological time, but the writers in this part seem to think in terms of more dynamic systems. Some embrace an accelerating pace of human-driven change as inevitable, even natural. When uncertainty troubles her young life, student Amy Coplen seeks context and comfort in shifts experienced by past generations. Definitions of wilderness as separate from human influence frustrate Lauren McCrady, who rejoices in the more complex, human-modified, semi-wild landscapes she has grown to love. Writers may question the rapid rate and sometimes dark trajectory of alteration, but they still find joy in the discoveries they make along the way. "The task ahead is to dismantle the boundaries we have constructed," writes Jason Brown, and then, with openness refreshed, "to watch what happens."

No one in *Coming of Age at the End of Nature* advocates sabotaging developers' earth-moving equipment as in Edward Abbey's novel *The Monkey Wrench Gang*, but the writers in part 3, "Mindful Monkeywrenching," offer creative solutions to diverse problems, both personal and societal. In "The Wager for Rain," Megan Kimble cannot find the science-based cure to drought she seeks but still rails against hope-less inertia, writing that "doing nothing is as much of an action as doing something." Several writers offer quotidian approaches to saving the world, from mopping floors to sporting Jordan high-tops in the wilderness. And Bonnie Frye Hemphill, while urging political action, asks perhaps the paramount question for all these young activists and change agents, however gentle or strident: "Will you join?"

Young adults care deeply about many issues, and the essays gathered here offer only a sampling. But the writings embody the truth of Henry David Thoreau's journal entry, written in 1852 when he was thirty-four: "All things in this world must be seen with the morning dew on them. Must be seen with youthful early-opened hopeful eyes." Careful readers of all ages will find in these pages early-opened phi-losophizing and practical advice, sweet hope, bitter recrimi-nations, dreams hazy and clear, but perhaps most of all, a rising will to do better.

PART I.
LIVING ON EAARTH

Post-Nature Writing

Blair Braverman

One summer, in college, I worked as a naturalist on a mountaintop in Aspen, Colorado. The mountaintop was a bustling place. A gondola emptied onto a gravel plain, where photographers in red polo shirts rushed to shoot each disembarking party. Behind them, an ornate lodge served customizable $14 stir-fries, and a short trail led downhill to a Frisbee golf course. There were beribboned Hula-Hoops lying around for anyone who wanted to hula, and sometimes there was a bungee trampoline set up for the kids, and sometimes a bluegrass band, and sometimes croquet, and sometimes a woman with a boa constrictor in a plastic tub that she let people touch with one finger. Occasionally she'd let me wear the boa around my neck, for naturalist cred.

I sat at a booth between the gondola and lodge with a painted sign that said "Ask a Naturalist!" People often took me up on the offer, but their questions were rarely nature-related. Did I happen to know the time? When was the last gondola down to the valley? If one went into the lodge, would one be obligated to buy food? I tried my best to be helpful.

Three times a day I stood on my stool and announced a short nature hike—a "hike," I always called it, though the distance was half a mile round trip and took less than an hour, going at a "naturalist's pace." I could usually persuade three or four good sports to venture out along the ridgeline, leaving the boa and bluegrass behind. I taught the differences between fir and pine, flax and phlox; I pointed out tiny alpine lupine and cinquefoil. We stopped at the decaying foundation of a miner's shack from the 1880s silver boom, snapped pictures, and passed into a pine grove where the walkers crossed their arms in the chill and I'd reach under squirrel mounds to pull out handfuls of hidden snow. The trail ended in a clearing with views on either side of the ridge. I led everyone to the left side, which looked down into a valley. It was green.

"Look at this view," I would say, as my boss had instructed me. "This is the same view that the silver miners saw 140 years ago. It's the same view that the Ute Indians saw 1,000 years ago." Then, lowering my voice: "And this land is protected, so it's the same view that people will see hundreds of years from now. When you look into this valley, you step outside your generation. You can see the past and the future at the same time."

It was a nice story. Even I thought it was nice. But it wasn't true.

I took people to the left side of the ridge because the right side told a different story. The land there was still protected, the valleys steep and uninhabited, with rocky cliffs and pine forests. But stretching from the far horizon, an orange shadow had begun to spread over the slopes. The pine bark beetle, a parasite brought to epidemic proportions due to a drought and climate change, had crossed the mountain West, leaving swathes of sick and dead lodgepole and ponderosa forest in its wake. Now that it had reached Aspen, no human could stop it from sweeping over the mountain and attacking the next valley. The view from the ridge may not have changed for a thousand years, but it would be changing soon.

I am part of a generation that grew up in the narrow window of the 1990s: young enough to learn about climate change in second-grade science class, but old enough not to get cell phones until high school. I spent much of my childhood playing with anthills and making frog houses out of mud, or sneaking into the bird sanctuary behind my parents' house to crouch in tall grass and spy on geese—the kind of childhood that is dying out, at least if the nostalgics are to be believed. And yet I was never not aware that nature was in collapse, that the woods I played in were fragmented and polluted, that the wolves in fairy tales were a kind of villain I was unlikely to encounter myself.

I don't remember the first time someone used the "grandchildren" line on me, but I was already familiar with it by the time—I must have been ten or so—when a classmate

spit her gum into a bush during recess and I, jealous of
the confidence with which she propelled the gum from
her pursed lips like a popped champagne cork, tried and
failed to do the same. The teacher spotted me with drool
and gum on my shoes and took the opportunity to teach
an afternoon lesson on littering. She raised pink fingernails
to her face, rubbing her temples as if unconsciously. "Don't
you want to keep the planet nice for your grandchildren
someday?" she said.

I would hear that line echoed throughout my adolescence
and college years. How would I want my grandchildren
to see me, as a hero or as a destroyer? Don't humans have
a duty to pass an unspoiled planet on to our grandchildren? How could we live with ourselves, delivering to our
grandchildren a world in such a state of disrepair? Just
ask James Hansen, the NASA scientist who in 1988—the
year I was born—testified before a congressional commit-
tee that global warming was the result of human activity,
and two decades later published *Storms of My Grandchildren*,
arguing that the planet—and the well-being of future generations—lay in "imminent peril." That means all of us, of
course, but once again, grandchildren stand in for all that
is innocent and suffering and hypothetical. Having com-
mitted no crimes of their own, our grandchildren—in the
silent springtime of their own lives—must reckon with an
inherited catastrophe.

Grandchildren! I am sick to death of those perfect forthcoming grandchildren. You know what? I am a grandchild,
an infant when Bill McKibben declared in 1989 that humans

had "stepped over the threshold" to the end of nature, and nobody has ever apologized to me.

Like the rest of my generation, I am no longer a hypothetical innocent sufferer; I am, rather, a cause of the problem, an inheritor of both the environmental crisis and the requisite senses of duty and guilt. "I didn't ask to be born!" whined Romanian philosopher Emil Cioran, and to that I'd like to add: I didn't ask to be born *now*. God, no. If I am responsible for my grandchildren's inheritance, then I'd like an apology from my grandparents, thank you, for destroying the species and open spaces I might have wished to share the planet with, or for the synthetic chemicals I've carried in my body since I was a fetus. But then again, why would they apologize? After all, I've also inherited all the benefits of our abusive globalized production system: the road trips and cheap computers, strawberries in December and nifty leaded-paint knick-knacks from China.

A friend asked a climate scientist what we should really do to prepare for climate change, and the scientist responded, "Teach your children to fight with knives." So maybe those children are the kids we should really apologize to, not me with my laptop and my melodrama. I didn't inherit a postapocalyptic world. Not yet, at least.

My employer in Colorado kept a library of nature books, and I snuck into the small room each morning to choose a book for the workday's downtime. I hadn't read much nature writing before, at least not intentionally, and associated the genre with textbooks and field guides. I remember the exact moment when I pulled the first book from the shelf—Annie Dillard's *Teaching a Stone to Talk*—and my eyes caught on the opening lines of one of the first essays: "A weasel is wild. Who knows what he thinks? He sleeps in his underground den, his tail draped over his nose. . . ."

I felt a sensation similar to one I'd had months earlier, during the first lecture of Environmental Studies 101, which I'd taken to fulfill a requirement. The lecture covered fisheries management. I had no interest in fisheries specifically, but I had tremendous interest, which I had never quite named or recognized, in how humans interact with their world. I sat very still in the third row, my heart racing. I felt a kind of desperate astonishment at having fallen into exactly the right place, one I hadn't known existed. It was almost frightening, in the way that falling in love is frightening—you can pretend, sure, but you're no longer in control.

Still holding the book, I don't think I fully exhaled until after the essay's final paragraph (" . . . it would be well, and proper, and obedient, and pure, to grasp your one necessity and not let it go . . . ") and by then I was late to the gondola and stuffed the book in my bag. I read the essay twice more that day and the rest of the book that night. Over the next weeks, I read Thoreau and Terry Tempest Williams, Rachel Carson and Ed Abbey and Rick Bass. Because I had not heard of most of the books, I didn't realize they were famous; because few other people seemed to use the library, I felt that I had discovered a secret that no one else knew.

But something didn't match up. The older books tended

to treat nature as if it were inherently perfect, and focused their energies on praise and description, or perhaps philosophizing about human relationships to the outdoors. The writers turned to nature to find solace and shelter from civilization, or because they were drawn to wildness, or both; nature was a place of awesomeness and respite, often at the same time.

From Arne Næss to Aldo Leopold, Ed Abbey to Thoreau, a great many of the older nature writers in the library—men in particular—took the time to go to the woods, and to diligently record the thoughts that occurred to them there. But over time, I found myself growing bored with their reverent prose, with their leisurely walks and months of contemplation. I took enough leisurely walks of my own, I didn't need to read about them, too. Despite my inclinations toward spending long days in the woods, or perching on boulders for hours, or—yes—exploring at a "naturalist's pace," I have no patience to read about others doing the same. I prefer statistics, analysis, calls to action. Even as I recognize the literary skill that goes into distilling a lonesome afternoon into three crisp paragraphs—complete with emotional setup, observation of biological phenomena, and tidy lesson—I prefer Rachel Carson's beautiful warnings and Sandra Steingraber's toxic science, David Gessner's schoolboy astonishment, and Annie Dillard's thrilling revulsion. I want drama and action.

Some might say that my impatience is generational, stemming from a childhood of flashing screens and instant messages; Næss would probably revoke my naturalist gig entirely. And sure, it's generational; I'll buy that. But my impatience—in this case, at least—is not the result of a carefully cultivated short attention span. It's a result of growing up with the overwhelming knowledge that we're running out of time. Leisurely, reverent nature writing made me uncomfortable, and since that summer, my discomfort has only grown. It feels indulgent to me, and blindered, like complimenting a friend's silky hair while she's being stabbed to death.

I could have taken the hikers to the valley on the right. I could have swept my arm over the creeping orange shadow, told them how the beetles bored into tree trunks and left them drafty as Swiss cheese, just like the silver miners had left the very mountain on which we were standing. I could have explained about the beetles leaving dead trunk after dead trunk, dead forest after dead forest, then moving to the next. I could have told the hikers about how the pheromone packets and pesticides and every other desperate attempt to stop the beetles had failed, because the only thing that could really stop them, the one thing that had always kept their population in check, was cold winters, and there simply weren't enough cold winters anymore. I could have told the hikers that, frankly, the beetles are the least of our problems. I could finally have let out my frustration with the quiet euphemisms of my elders, with their references to a "changing planet" rather than a "planet gone to fuck."

But I didn't. I didn't even let myself think about giving

that talk, because then I would have had to answer to myself, to why I didn't. Every day I led the tour group past the log cabin, through the cool forest, and out onto the ridge, and every day I steered them to the left and stood back for the gasps. The view never failed to elicit gasps. And the gasps were wonderful. They warmed me; they rose like bubbles. I was hooked on them. For a few minutes, standing there on the ridge over the green valley, surrounded by people who believed it, I could almost imagine I was looking into something pure.

Why Haiti?

Elizabeth Cooke

Why Haiti? I answer this question endlessly.

There's the personal angle: Why did I go to Haiti? My rambling response mentions the Haitian student my parents sponsored at a Midwest university, the Miami-based biodiesel fanatic my dad met online, and the California foundation that funded my fellowship to work in the small Caribbean nation.

Then there's the universal angle: Why does disaster stalk Haiti? Hurricanes, earthquakes, famine, unrest. Why are these the country's headlines? This question is trickier. Entire books have been written about the topic, searching for the historical, political, ecological, and cultural reasons why.

I don't claim to have the answer to this second question. I only have my experience, the personal, which together with many millions of others' experiences combine like the dots in a pointillist painting to make up a portrait of Haiti.

I pick at the food on my plate while mosquitoes feast on my ankles. It's my first day in Haiti, and anxiety has sent my appetite fleeing. I don't want to appear rude, so I chat with Georges, the biodiesel fanatic who's serving as my fellowship mentor, and Pastor Michel, the founder of the evangelical mission that's hosting me. They make an odd couple. Georges, Haitian by birth but an American citizen, is agnostic in all matters other than biofuel. Pastor Michel, a lifelong Haitian, is a devout Christian. Together, though, they've taken up a crusade to reverse what they both agree is the sinful destruction of Haiti's trees. I'm here to help.

Exhausted by the long day of travel, I'm debating whether it's too early to excuse myself and retreat to my bedroom when Georges sets down his utensils and announces we have a meeting to attend. We move upstairs, where we join three local agronomists sitting in a circle on wicker chairs. Georges shares his dream of a day when Haitian women and children will no longer cook over the smoky, asthma-inducing charcoal fires that have, tree by tree, stripped the nation's mountains bare. He prophesies a verdant Haiti where oil-producing trees, such as castor and *Jatropha curcas*, will provide clean-burning fuel, preserve the country's eroding soils, and slow the floodwaters that rush down the naked slopes.

His words are inspiring, but they're not easy to put into practice, as I discover when he returns to Miami a few days later, leaving me with an abandoned nursery, a musty store-room full of jumbled tools, and a broad swathe of dusty land that, he tells me, is mine to plant from one mountain chain to the next. At that moment, I'm struck by the yawning gap that exists between ambitious, world-changing visions and the backbreaking, tedious work required to realize them.

I've been in Haiti less than a month, and I'm already doubt-ing my decision to come. I feel lost and lonely—and use-less. Native Creole sounds nothing like the audio lessons I listened to back home, and Haitian French is a far cry from the Parisian French I studied in school. It's a major accom-plishment when I manage to buy an avocado.

To top it all off, the mission is hosting a summer camp. The place is swarming with children who delight in try-ing to extract gifts from the young *"blan."* Boys who've just eaten their afternoon meal pat their bellies and cry out *"Mwen grangou!"* while girls follow me around asking for my skirt, my watch, my shoes.

One evening, after planting seeds with the children and their camp teachers, I splash a handful of water on my sweaty, sunscreen-slick face, then collapse on my bed and pray for a breeze to sway the curtains. Lying there, I think back to the wintry Wisconsin evening when I first hatched the idea to work in Haiti. It was a crystal clear night. A translucent moon hung high in the indigo sky, and as I strapped on my mom's skis and set out across the fields, gliding over four-foot snowdrifts, I felt weightless, limitless, unbound.

I was so certain back then that I had something to gain—something to give—by moving to Haiti. All I had to do was leap and trust I'd land safely on the other side. Now that I'm here, though, I'm not so certain anymore. Why me? Why Haiti? God only knows.

I lean against the ruined ramparts of Fort-Liberté, an old colonial stronghold on the northern coast of Haiti, as the last light from the setting sun plays across the waves below. At my side is the mission's kindergarten teacher, Cherline, who has made a particular effort to befriend me despite my faltering French and nearly nonexistent Creole.

We're here for a long weekend, accompanying Pastor Michel on business and taking the opportunity to escape the noise and crowds of Gonaïves, the port city where the mission is based. It's quieter and calmer, easier to see the lingering beauty of the island here in this sleepy seaside town. In both places, though, the ghosts of Haiti's past lurk.

They're present in the fort itself, a crumbling landmark from the days when the French got rich off this land through a system of brutal slavery and rapacious plantation farming. They're present in the central square of Gonaïves, where Haitian slaves first declared their independence and where subsequent generations have marched against native-born dictators and foreign interveners alike. They're present in the shiny new aid trucks, T-shirts, and billboards, the latest manifestation of a centuries-long American effort to refashion this country, including a nineteen-year military occupation. And they're present in the vanishingly small plots of land where many Haitians scrape out a living while those in power scrabble over the thin cream at the top.

No amount of murmuring from these ghosts, however, can ruin this evening. Cherline and I lay our heads on our arms and close our eyes, savoring the soft sea breezes and the sound of the waves lapping at the rocks.

"Quel est le mot pour 'vent' en anglais?" asks Cherline. I open my eyes and find hers on me.

"Wind," I tell her and ask for the word in Creole.

We continue to trade words in English and Creole, using French as our medium. Sea. Clouds. Sky. Moon. Stars. As night closes in, purple flashes of distant lightning turn the mountains into a spectacular landscape of light and shadow, their grandeur undiminished by their surface scars.

I'm still not sure exactly why I'm here, but I'm glad I am.

Soon after our return to Gonaïves, a series of hurricanes sweep across the island, transforming the roads into quagmires and bringing our tree-planting efforts to a halt.

"Elizabeth! Elizabeth!" cries Cherline outside my door late one night, startling me awake. I grapple with the mosquito net over my bed and swing my feet to the floor. They land in water.

"It's okay," says Cherline when I open the door. "Don't be scared." We stand there for a moment, face to face in the flickering light of her kerosene lamp, then get to work.

Shuffling through the ankle-deep water, we move clothes, food, books—everything we can—to high shelves before hauling two twin mattresses up to the creaky second floor.

The wind howls through the cracks in the walls, and the rain drums against the tin roof. I curl up on my mattress, thinking of the people on lower ground who must be fleeing for their lives as the ocean surges and the rivers burst their banks. Cherline paces next to me, trying to get calls through on her cell phone to family and friends.

Neither of us sleeps.

In the gray light of morning, we wade outside through knee-high water, the wind whipping the rain into our faces. My green hiking pack is strapped to my back, and Cherline holds my arm as we move slowly forward, feeling for hidden branches or ruts in the road. The water streams across the land, rippling where it dips into ditches. We move a little faster as we pass under an uprooted tree dangling from another tree's branches.

Around us, hundreds of people carry mattresses, cooking pots, clothes, and other essentials to higher ground. Most move into the mission school just up the road. The scene is sobering, but no one has yet grasped the full scale of the disaster. Instead, there is a sense of adventure and vitality and community as neighbors wave and shout greetings.

Pastor Michel laughs jovially when he spots Cherline and me from his front porch, declaring me the great American explorer. I'm happy to provide him with comic relief. He'll need it in the coming days.

Make it stop, I think, covering my ears and squeezing my eyes shut. It's the third night of constant, pounding rain, and the sense of adventure has long since worn off. Hundreds of people drowned that first night, trapped in low-lying areas where there was no chance for escape, and widespread flooding has isolated thousands more. Hunger is starting to set in. And another hurricane is on the way.

As I lie in the darkness, willing it all to stop, the unexpected sound of singing cuts through the rain. It's coming from the next room over, where a dozen girls are draped across chairs and stretched out on the cement floor. The older girls, I slowly realize, are soothing the fears of the younger ones with familiar hymns. From song, they shift into prayer. Each girl says her own. Aloud. Simultaneously. The rhythmic prayers form a new type of song that is percussive, hypnotic, lulling.

As a fallen-away Catholic, I am sometimes skeptical of religious ritual, but if there were ever a time for calling on God's mercy, this is it. And this seems to be a good way of going about it.

"We're heading downtown," says Cherline. "Bring your camera."

The hurricanes have finally blown over, and the sun is trying to break through the clouds. I'm not sure what we'll find in the city center, but I readily agree to go. The encroaching water has made the mission feel like a shrinking island, and I want to reassure myself that there's life beyond its borders.

We push Pastor Michel's old beater of an SUV until the engine turns over, then cram inside. Four of us take the backseat, and another two climb into the rear cargo hold. One young man scrambles onto the roof just before we pull out of the mission gates.

On our way into the city, we pass a long line of people wading out with bundles on their heads. The water extends clear to the base of the mountains, making a lake out of farm fields, and as I listen to the car's motor chug reluctantly through it, I start to question the sanity of driving deeper into the devastation.

Gonaïves is a ruined city. Brown water ripples, swells, and pools everywhere. Snapped power lines snake through the windows of an overturned school bus, and skeletal dogs crouch on muddy atolls in the rivers that used to be streets. We stop on a small rise, and I watch solemnly as crowds of people trudge through the watery wreckage.

Some shout. Some laugh. Some cry. But most are silent, their eyes vacant. This can't be happening, those empty eyes seem to say. This can't be real.

The water has turned green. Mosquitoes flourish in the stagnant pools, and the smell would be unbearable if there were any choice but to bear it. It's a nauseating mixture of everything that has been submerged and is now rotting— animal carcasses, human waste, heaps of trash. At night, cool breezes drift over the water and through the windows. They should be refreshing but instead leave me gasping like a fish for a breath that isn't quite there.

The days are busy. Meetings are held with community leaders. Reports are prepared for donors. Calls are made to coordinate supply drops. One morning, I discover a visitor sitting on Pastor Michel's front steps. He smiles and stands when he sees me, wiping his hand on his trousers before reaching out to shake mine.

It's Dumond, one of the agronomists I met my first night in Haiti, and who has worked closely with me on the tree-planting project. I haven't seen him since the torrents hit. I give him a summary of the damage, telling him that all of the seedlings in the nursery are gone, lost in the flooding. Then we track down a key to the storeroom and head across the mission, at times traversing by rooftop to avoid the murky lake that has formed around the edges of the place.

Dumond stops at the bottom of a set of stairs to roll up his pants and tells me to stay where I am. He hesitates only a second before stepping into the tea-green water. I sit down to wait, listening to his sloshing footsteps as he wades to the storeroom door. When he returns, he hauls a heavy sack to the roof and spreads a few seeds in the sun, cracking them open to smell for rot. He picks out two handfuls to save, seed by seed, then heaves the sack to the edge of the roof and dumps the rest into the water.

This marks the end of our first attempt at Georges's dream.

"Do you like the Haitian nature?" a young man named Sadrack asks me.

We're sitting on a cement wall, waiting our turn at the local well. I hesitate, trying to decide what he means. Do I like the personality of the Haitian people? Or do I like the country's landscape? I decide he means the latter and reply, "Yes."

Sadrack asks me why.

"The mountains," I say. "They're beautiful. Of course, they should have more trees. But still, they're beautiful. And the ocean. That's beautiful, too."

I pause, wondering if my words sound as hollow to Sadrack as they do to me. Most of the time, when I look at the bare mountains or the dirty harbors, I can't help wondering how they looked when the Taino people lived here, before Columbus discovered this "New World." Tonight, though, the mountains really are beautiful. The moon, one sliver short of full, hovers above their rocky peaks, and the setting sun reflects off their slopes, creating a lovely tableau of light and shadow just as I saw on that night in Fort-Liberté with Cherline.

"Someday, when I have a family," says Sadrack, "I'll take them up to the mountains every weekend. We'll camp away from the city. Smelling the fresh air. Eating the fruits of Haiti—mangos, bananas, coconuts. I've gone camping with the Boy Scouts. I liked it."

I nod. I'm intrigued. Six months have passed since the hurricanes, and many people have still not returned to their homes. In fact, canvas refugee shelters are set up in rows on a dusty plain just down the road from where Sadrack and I sit. He's the first Haitian I've met who aspires to getting into a tent, not out of one.

"But you need money to live like that," he continues, turning melancholy. "You need a job. I'll probably never even get married. I have to support my parents. My life is already over."

"You're young," I tell him. "Life can change."

"Not my life."

I want to say this isn't true, but who am I to make that call?

I grip the hard seat of a moto while the driver maneuvers expertly between trucks, goats, and bicycles. We're on our way to Passe Reine, a small mountain community that wants to help with the reforestation project.

After a breathtaking thirty-minute ride over roller-coaster roads, we rumble to a stop and Pastor Josué from the mission pulls up behind us. We're greeted by a local leader who guides us, on foot, up a series of winding switch-backs to a high, scrubby plain. A few dozen people are hacking at the brush with machetes, singing as they work, but they stop at the sight of us and gather round to hear what we have to say.

I offer a few words in hesitant Creole about my hopes for the project, then Pastor Josué speaks at greater length, tes-tifying to his faith that the hurricanes, terrible though they were, present an opportunity to build a greener, healthier, more vibrant country. His words contrast starkly with those of another pastor in Gonaïves who distributed fliers after the storms declaring that they were God's retribution for Haiti's pact with the devil.

When Pastor Josué is finished, several people come up to me and tug at my arm, pointing to the surrounding slopes.

"We can plant there," they say.

"And there."

"And on my land over there."

Perhaps, I decide, there's space left yet for dreaming.

I stand at the end of a deserted road where it trails off into the hurricane lake that once was farmers' fields. Birds swoop low over the water, landing in dead treetops to scan for fish or frogs, while occasional gusts of wind send ripples across the glassy surface. It's a lake that should not exist, that would not, arguably, if the mountains were lush with trees. But then, there are many parts of Haiti that, in theory, should not exist, and when it comes to casting blame for the tragedies of this place, it's easy to point fingers.

Why Haiti?

Because of the French.

Because of the Americans.

Because of the elites.

Because of the masses.

Because of our sins.

Whether there's some special cosmic punishment or reward lined up for this particular plot of earth, I don't know. All I know is that the wind and the water, the fish and the frogs, the people in tents and the people in palaces—Haiti and I—are here together witnessing this moment in time and shaping the next.

And for now, that's answer enough.

Rebuild or Retreat

Is It Time to Give Up on Places Like the Rockaways?

Ben Goldfarb

In May 2012, my girlfriend Elise and I ventured out for the first time to the Rockaways, the narrow finger of beach that stands like a bodyguard between New York City and the Atlantic Ocean. The water was still too cold for swimming, but the spring day was warm enough to justify soggy paper cups of lemon-flavored shaved ice, which melted down our wrists as we wandered along the iconic boardwalk. As surfers skated across gentle rollers and shorebirds scurried in the wash, we voiced our delight and disbelief: how could such a serene and lovely place exist in the same city as Midtown Manhattan?

We didn't return to the Rockaways until mid-November, and the scene then could not have been more different: instead of strolling along the boardwalk, we found ourselves excavating ruined chunks of it from people's front yards. The peninsula, of course, had borne the brunt of "Superstorm Sandy," and three weeks later the area remained devastated, its residents forced to contend with no power, no heat, and, most ignominiously, Long Island's sewage. Currents carried the effluent from Nassau County's damaged treatment plants right past Rockaway Beach. The situation was so bad that Doctors Without Borders, a humanitarian group that typically operates in chronically distressed countries like Haiti and Sierra Leone, showed up on American soil for the first time to rescue elderly people trapped in their apartments. For three weeks, the chorus from the neglected barrier island had been some variation of "Where's the help?!"—with an expletive usually inserted between the second and third words, this being Queens.

While Elise and I, on our return visit, expected a near-anarchic hinterland—the Free Republic of the Rockaways, as *New York Magazine* put it—the reality turned out to be more complex, though not necessarily less dire. The cavalry had arrived, even if it was unforgivably slow in coming. Dump trucks and heavy machinery bearing the insignia of the Department of Sanitation scooped up mountains of rubble from the streets. Electricians in the baskets of cherry pickers disentangled snarled power lines every third block. And vast armies of volunteers, from the Occupy Sandy movement to Seventh-Day Adventists to Bill Clinton, had come to pick up garbage and dispense supplies.

Even as the power blinked back on and the mangled cars vanished from the sidewalks, the Rockaways still faced a challenge that seemed truly intractable: the vast drifts of sand that the storm surge had lifted off the beach and dumped in the basements and yards of hundreds of ocean-front homes. We found one such house easily enough, guided by a square of plywood, propped against a nest of ruined bicycles, with the words "Help Needed" scrawled in green marker across its face. In the dank basement, a trio of Occupy Sandy volunteers stripped busted pipes and shoveled away the last of the sand. "Finally hit solid ground yesterday morning," grunted a volunteer named Ryan as she emerged up the concrete stairs, her face smudged with grit, "and it was like, thank God—there *is* a floor!"

In the front yard of the home, the sand situation was still critical. Towering wet berms of the stuff had been hurled up against the house next door, blocking its owners from getting inside. For three hours we hacked away at the drifts with shovels, relocating hundreds of pounds of sand from the smothered yard to the curb for Sanitation to haul away. Our efforts felt as much archaeological as restorative: entombed within the huge dunes was the detritus of doz-ens of lives, artifacts that Sandy had swept from roads and beaches and deposited here, just west of Ninetieth Street, just north of Shore Front Parkway. Our shovels overturned the bricks of a patio, shards of chimneys, strips of siding, butterfly nets. A faded photo of two boys on a seesaw, squinting at the camera in bright morning light. Sections of steel pipes, light fixtures, a toy horse, the inevitable condom. "At least somebody's using 'em," quipped a volunteer named Meredith.

Roving gangs of hipster videographers dressed in flannel

jackets and fur-lined hoods sidled up and furtively shot video as we shoveled. A workman in a hard hat, who had driven four days from Denver to help turn the gas back on, strolled over and snapped a few pictures. A film crew from the Red Cross shot some tape and then asked us, please, would we mind taking a break from our work to just sign these release forms allowing them to use the footage in halftime commercials that would air during Thanksgiving football games? Just sign here . . . and here . . . and on the reverse side, right here.

We signed, and got back to digging, the endless movement of sand from this pile *here* to this pile over *there*, the job both fulfilling and futile. Up and down Shore Front there was sand and more sand, dunes and waves and drifts, the air hazy and pale with grit storms kicked up by the wailing fire trucks that barreled through intersections strung with still-dark traffic lights.

By 1 P.M., we had unearthed most of the backyard, and we began to hit soil. My shovel flipped over a bulb, just starting to sprout; Elise unearthed a clump of green onions that smelled like spring in her palm. The home's owner, a woman named Mary, appeared from around the side of the house, a gray ponytail dangling beneath her baseball hat. "Sorry I've got you working out here like it's the Middle Ages," she called as she approached. She stood before us and gazed down at the plants in our palms.

"Looks like you've found my garden," she said, more amazed than mournful. Mary gestured to a choked cluster of dead branches poking from the top of a new sand dune.

"That was my lilac." She picked up the broken fronds of what looked like a cedar. "My little evergreen." A brown twisted vine ran across the sand and grabbed at our ankles. "And that's a twenty-year-old wisteria." Decades to grow, hours to kill.

We asked her if she wanted to save the bulbs and replant them. She sighed and rolled one in her hand. "Nah, don't think I will," she said. Still, she didn't throw the bulb away—instead, she laid it carefully on a plastic table strewn with her belongings, as if she might just change her mind.

Since Sandy howled up the East Coast, there has been plenty of discussion about how to prevent such a disaster from repeating itself, most of it focused on infrastructural improvements. Should the city restore the wetlands and oyster beds that once fringed Manhattan? Create absorptive streets capable of swallowing incoming waves? Construct massive tidal gates across the East River, Arthur Kill, and Verrazano-Narrows? Invariably, it seems, these proposals are dismissed as inadequate, or impossible, or prohibitively expensive.

Another "re-" word, however, has joined the ranks of restoration, resilience, and reconstruction in the conversation about New York's options, and this one is even more radical: retreat.

Most scientific modeling suggests that while run-of-the-mill hurricanes may not become more common in coming years, climate change will spawn ultra-destructive super-storms more frequently. Add giant storms to higher sea levels and it appears that Sandy represents not an isolated disaster, but an early salvo in climate change's assault on our coastlines.

Knowing that places like the Rockaways lie squarely in harm's way, should we encourage people like Mary to reconstruct their homes at all? For decades, the federal government has been doing just that through its FEMA-administered National Flood Insurance Program, which provides money for people to rebuild in the wake of catastrophic flooding. And while this generosity is surely appreciated by communities sitting along coasts and upon floodplains, it has led to some truly shortsighted decisions: as the *New York Times* reported in 2012, taxpayers have spent $80 million since 1979 reconstructing houses and bridges on tiny Dauphin Island in Alabama, even though the island gets hit by hurricanes roughly every three years.

What's more, the people living in the riskiest places don't necessarily pay higher premiums. Since 1988, for example, Dauphin Island's residents have received $72.2 million in flood relief, but paid only $9.3 million. That's why whenever the nation is hit by particularly destructive events, such as Hurricane Katrina in 2005, the flood insurance program finds itself deeply in the red. Thanks to Sandy, 2012 was the program's worst year for claims since Katrina; as of 2014, the program stood $24 billion in debt.

Consequently, reforming, or even disbanding, the flood insurance program has become the rare cause célèbre capable of uniting environmentalists and libertarians. Groups like SmarterSafer advocate eliminating the subsidies that keep flood insurance premiums artificially low, and creating actuarial tables for coastal areas that better reflect flood risk. "No federal dollars should magically appear for rebuilding in flood-prone areas," wrote marine biologist Carl Safina in the weeks after the storm. "The spots that flood will take repeated hits. Everyone knows this. To help people rebuild in those places is to help put lives and investment in harm's way. It's foolish."

Of course, without the program's largesse providing a backstop, lots of places, from the Outer Banks to New Orleans to perhaps the Rockaways, may become virtually uninhabitable for all but the wealthiest homeowners. Private insurers perceive flood insurance as too risky to offer, and without insurance, it doesn't make a whole lot of sense to build on unstable, wave-vulnerable barrier islands. Many people will have little choice but to retreat inland.

There's no question that if doing the same thing over and over and expecting different results is the definition of insanity, thoughtlessly rebuilding communities in low-lying coastal areas is certifiably nuts. As George Carlin said of people who refuse to budge from midwestern floodplains, "They repaint, put down new carpeting and wallpaper, and they move right back into the same [bleeping] house on the floodplain, next to the river . . . and then they wonder why Grandma's floating downstream with the parakeet on her head!" The National Flood Insurance Program needs to be drastically reformed, and the perverse incentives it creates to repeatedly reconstruct homes and buildings that are doomed from the instant that their first brick is laid need to be eliminated. We must change the way we conceptualize our relationship with the coast, to recognize its risks as clearly as we do its rewards. Inevitably, that will mean letting some places slip into the rising seas.

Still, as I watched Mary direct the volunteers scurrying about her ruined home, her resolve to rebuild already etched in her face, the implications of abandoning the Rockaways and other coastal zones gnawed at me. What hazard-free cities and states—if such places even exist—would accept thousands of domestic refugees with open arms? What culture will be lost if the Rockaways, and other risk-prone settlements, slip away? What will happen to the psyches of the Rockaway Peninsula residents, already among New York City's poorest and most marginalized people, if they're scattered to the winds? And what about their counterparts across the country, and the world? Who will take them in, and at what cost?

Winter Solstice

Lisa Hupp

Hope is not that thing with feathers. Rather, it springs forward on furred feet in teasing loops and crisscrossing paths, always one or two moves ahead of my single-minded chocolate Lab puppy. She presses her nose into the snowy tracks and faithfully traces back and forth under spruce trees and salmonberry bushes, never catching but ever in pursuit.

Today is a rare windless winter day on Kodiak and I am out to celebrate the extra minute of sunlight due to us. It is the day after solstice, that tipping point of winter when vitamin-deficient Alaskans turn their faces south to the horizon and worship the slow return of the sun, convincing themselves that the next five months of winter will be bearable because each day will be lighter than the last.

My boots shuffle through the powdery drifts of a cold and recent snow. The forest muffles my steps and mutes the cackle of a raven high above. Small creeks run black and echo under ice bridges and around mossy roots. Lily the Lab races out ahead, reading the daily journal of the forest floor: the slingshot prints of snowshoe hares, the elegant and slight pounce of an ermine. The long and industrious track of a beaver slide carves down the hillside of thorny wild rose bushes and into a frozen pond. Sitka black-tailed deer step warily in search of winter browse; the feathery brush of a large wing marks the bloody end of a ground squirrel. A red fox has run through here recently, the paw prints slightly smaller than those of my dog.

Out of long habit, I've kept an eye out for the large pad with diagonal toes and lightly imprinted claw tips. Not from a particular fear, but simply because it is the thing to do when living on an island with 3,000 brown bears: keep awareness, respect the other, and above all, avoid the element of surprise.

On this archipelago of rocky islands in the North Pacific Ocean, the Kodiak brown bear has a distinction that goes beyond its size and charisma. It is one of the few animals here that indisputably belongs to its place. Genetic studies trace bears on Kodiak back nearly to the end of the last ice age in Southwest Alaska, between 10,000 and 12,000 years ago. Only five other creatures can lay a similar claim; the rest have settled as pioneers unwittingly carrying out a kind of manifest destiny. Aerial missions to trap and introduce mountain goats in the 1950s for "roasts and rugs" succeeded fabulously; deer, elk, beaver, and snowshoe hares came earlier in the century for similar reasons. As transplants go, they've blended in well—most people have forgotten that there was a time when their tracks didn't pattern the snow.

It is another winter day, probably near the solstice, and I am ten years old. The immense landscape has a predawn hush and the truck's heater fights with a snapping cold outside. The earth falls away up here. My father likes to point out the way its shadow curves, gray-purple on the edge of the sky right after sunset. This is one of my most distinct memories: he wakes me up in the dark, and we drive along twisting mountain roads until we've climbed so high that the walls of snow on either side seem to swallow us up, quiet and sleepy and watchful.

We finally crest up into a bowl of sky that is still and clear and all shades of night. Balanced on the rim of the crater, we can look out over a blue-black lake and beyond into the plateaus east of the Cascade Range. We are waiting for a full moon to set and the sun to rise over the volcanic remains of Mount Mazama. My father hopes to photograph an ancient white pine twisting against the winter sky. I'm just along for the ride, one part witness and two parts captive audience on the receiving end of lectures about composition and exposures. As a gold glow begins to limn the eastern crater rim, my breath puffs and hangs in wonder.

I grew up thinking of these predawn trips and places as completely normal. My parents both worked for the U.S. Forest Service, and the public lands and forests of the Pacific Northwest were like one big backyard, with national marvels like the Hoh Rain Forest and Crater Lake just a short drive away from our tiny communities of natural resource agency and industry folk. In elementary school we learned to core and age trees; after school I wasn't allowed indoors until dinnertime. In third grade I made friends with a girl who had just moved from a big city somewhere in Arizona. Mystified by my ignorance of all things cool, she had to explain Cabbage Patch dolls, boom boxes, and New Kids on the Block.

Later, when we moved into a larger town and I went to high school, the defense against my lack of pop culture knowledge started all over again. "It's because your parents are hippies," my classmates said. And I would think, sure, we own a fruit dehydrator and have more than one Janis Joplin record. But, hippies? Somehow there were never the right words to describe what filled in the gaps of my childhood, like the way my mother took us to visit a defunct fire lookout and showed how she used to stand on a glass-footed stool to escape stray electric current during lightning storms, or how my father went on backcountry ski expeditions and brought back Kodachrome slides of red tents lit up at night and untracked snowfields under the stars.

My father first read me Aldo Leopold's "Thinking like a Mountain" when I was eight years old and infatuated with wolves. I discovered "The Land Ethic" twelve years later, while pining for all things West in a vaulted reading room of the Bodleian Library at Oxford. "A thing is right," Leopold wrote, "when it tends to preserve the integrity, stability, and beauty of the biotic community." And I thought, yes, this is the homage that we attempted daily to live within forests of cedar, hemlock, and fir.

Leopold led to other stories of wild and backyard places. Here, I thought, I've found my people. Especially in writers who cultivated my homesickness for the Northwest: Gary Snyder, in a poem about the Elwha River in the Olympic Mountains; David James Duncan describing the rain in the Oregon Coast Range. Their writings were like a series of love letters etching out personal landscapes of home and belonging and the wonders of the natural world.

An environmental justice seminar during my senior year brought a new set of voices into this academic study of place. I read about the displacement of people from their homes for the sake of a reservoir big enough to supply the city of Boston, about uranium mining and cancer in the Nevada desert, and about the ecology of toxins. Six of us sat in a brick tower on a beautiful East Coast campus discussing Sandra Steingraber's book about the accumulation of PCBs in the human body and asked ourselves: how do we live in such a broken world?

Throughout that class, I'm ashamed to admit I took some comfort in knowing that there were places of refuge like the Olympic Mountains and Crater Lake—perpetually protected and inviolate. My home was safe, surely, from the desolation I studied. Not that I didn't recognize the degradation associated with resource extraction throughout the Pacific Northwest. I had lived in logging towns and seen plenty of clear-cuts. But the places of my childhood seemed too large, too steep, too remote for any kind of permanent damage.

Then one day we read an essay by Steingraber, and my sense of security suffered blunt force trauma. Poisonous dioxin produced in U.S. industry, I read, travels on prevailing winds up to the eastern arctic and Greenland, deposits, accumulates in wildlife and humans, and then concentrates in the breast milk of Inuit mothers at levels several times higher than American women.

Somehow this was the ultimate betrayal. Apparently I had been wrong. No place was safe, not even the vastness of Greenland. Not even the deep blue of a lake in an abandoned volcanic crater, high in Cascade Mountains. Vulnerability cracked through and I thought differently about all those love letters written to places, written to *my* places: the words became elegies, tinged with despair and loss.

It's winter again. A January snowstorm after midnight. The wind is gusting more than sixty miles an hour, but we're still working outside on the deck of this Russian ship. Rime ice hangs inside a cavernous freezer hatch, three stories deep. I concentrate on the click of the hydraulic gears; a second too late, and I'll end up missing the narrow opening and splattering frozen cod all the way down to C deck. It's my third season working with this crew of men at the end of the world, and I'm still nervous about making a mistake.

This island is unforgiving in so many ways. It is the only

bit of land between Hawaii and the Bering Sea, and the cold scrapes over smooth white hills without hesitation.

After college I found that I couldn't see the places of my childhood in the same way and so I moved on to that next-west place, with even greater wilderness, with communities even more remote. At the time it was a barely conscious decision—impetuously answering an ad for dockworkers in the Aleutian Islands after spending my summer on a fire crew in Idaho. It was winter, and I had used up all of my fire money looking for work in Missoula. I grasped at the thread of Alaska with both hands.

The Aleutians didn't disappoint. There were wide swaths of rye grass and wild iris in the summers, craggy beaches in every direction, and even active volcanoes. But there were no trees, and at the end of the spring I ended up on another island in the North Pacific, another former World War II outpost with an economy based on commercial fishing, government agencies, and the odd tourist.

Kodiak's forest is different from the one where I grew up—an island monoculture of Sitka spruce on the very tail end of a temperate rainforest that stretches north and west from the rainy side of the Cascades. But the cling of moss, the green-gold color of the sun filtering down, and the understory of blueberries and devil's club are familiar enough, and here I have lived for the past seven years.

Like all small towns, Kodiak has dynasties that can trace their legacy down a family tree rooted in place: third-generation fishers whose grandfathers came here from Norway; families with Russian last names who can trace their grandmother's grandmother back to an Alutiiq village. And then there's us. The transients, the seasonal workers, the ones who came here from somewhere else, looking for who knows what—a job, an adventure, a close encounter with wildlife. Chasing the myth of Alaska-the-last-frontier.

I would hold my right hand on *Walden* and swear to you that I didn't believe in that myth. That I knew better (remember Greenland?). That I wasn't chasing anything when I drifted in from the Aleutians for a summer job as a backcountry park ranger, and ended up spending the winter.

It was never a choice to stay—just a decision not to leave.

Kodiak isn't the easiest place to set up house. The cost of living is high, the weather is harsh, and the plane tickets to warmer places are expensive. But there is something about it that catches and holds. Maybe it is the sheer expanse—walking from end to end would take a person more than three weeks, if they knew how: how to bushwhack through tangled thickets of alders and berry bushes, how to move across sheer slopes and glacial rivers. It would take someone months or years—a lifetime, maybe—to claim more than a glancing acquaintance with this island.

My past seven years have been a patchwork of exploration and a bid for belonging in this community. A summer commercial salmon fishing, a job inventorying contaminated World War II sites for a tribal council, and a year spent going through boxes of fuel receipts and electrical bills, crunching carbon footprint numbers for the local munici-

pal government. Has the bid been successful? I work for
Kodiak National Wildlife Refuge now, part of an agency
with a mission to protect and conserve. I talk to people
about the native mammals, about the spine-tingling awe of
watching bears catching fish at a waterfall, about endangered whales that migrate past our coasts.

Every summer, a new group of students arrives from
just about everywhere other than Alaska. They come to the
refuge to practice college skills in biology and environmental education, to be part of a place that *protects* and *conserves*.
Invariably, their application essays express a desire to do
meaningful work in conservation. To research wildlife in
their natural habitat, to experience a wilderness adventure,
to save something worth saving. For three or four months
each year I soak in their optimism and energy, their ideal-
ism. They move on in the fall, to the next park or refuge
or reserve, leaving me eight long months of winter to reflect
on the dubious privilege of living their exotic adventure as
a full-time job.

Here is the hard part: I've just about run out of west.
This island is one big "end of land sadness." And that
scares the hell out of me. It takes courage to love a place,
to deliberately choose digging in and taking responsibility
for its fragile well-being. Recognizing the magnitude of our
impact on the community of life that sustains us means
coming to terms with fear, loss, and degrees of despair.

I honestly don't know if I have what it takes to stay for
the long haul. Almost a decade after getting my heart broken by dioxin, I can't look at the wild beauty of this coast-

line without also seeing the rainbow-colored plastic piles of marine debris that wash up on the beaches. The bone-white fins of Kodiak's first wind turbines tilt on the hillside above town, but our local politicians still can't agree about the reality of climate change. Most of this island is a federal refuge, but the migrating birds and fish that depend on its habitat also depend on the health of a wider, unprotected environment.

I recently saw a photograph of Kodiak taken from space. It was winter. The archipelago spread out from north to south, a white fringe of lace in a black sea. As I looked closer, I could pick out the individual bays and fjords that radiate out from a central spine. To the west: Uganik Bay, where I sat on the porch of a cabin with friends this past summer, drinking beer and watching the sun set over fields of bright fireweed and distant glaciers of the Katmai mountains. Their infant daughter slept inside, not yet aware of the daily rhythms at fish camp. To the north: Shuyak. The island where I spent my first summer, learning to solo kayak in the company of an inquisitive seal on quiet waters at dawn. To the south: a river I hiked along in the early morning fog. Moisture hung on every lupine leaf, and the wary outline of a bear stalked along the opposite bank.

It's January. This morning I woke up to the low angle of a winter sun after weeks of grumbling rain. Lily and I walked our daily trail up the ridge, through moss-hung spruce and swampy puddles. This afternoon, I began looking through a new batch of student applications. Over the next few days I will read about their desire to come to

Alaska, their passion for working outside in terrible weather and biting insects, and their ideals for a career in wildlife conservation. I'll think about what I want so badly to keep, about the kind of world that I want for my friends' young sons and daughters. And I'll hope.

Urban Foraging

Amaris Ketcham

We've got tricks to get grub. We've specialized. We convene and share our food. We're underemployed—staffers at local nonprofits because we believe in a more sustainable future with our hearts in the right places. And nonprofits know how to take advantage of youth.

A white girl I know works with the homeless, and she has to cash in food stamps because her paychecks don't cover the full cost of living under a roof. She wants to be social, though, like a normal twenty-three-year-old, and she believes in fostering a sense of community, so she hosts potluck-style "Sunday Night Dinners" with standing, open invitations. She's got interesting tastes, and she always buys products like prosciutto and ciabatta bread to add to the array and to show us what these foods are like. Each week, we can share our food and eat her food stamps, too.

One of my male friends works for a door-to-door politics information and donation-solicitation company. He gets paid for each donor signed, works sixty hours a week, and barely makes rent. So he got a side-job cleaning out foreclosures and evictions, and his boss is kind enough to let the guys keep the food from the pantries. They divvy up the goods after each job. Last week, he made a windfall: a bomb shelter in a basement with ten-pound bags of freeze-dried food. Each morning, he's been breakfasting on a cup of dehydrated bananas, or, as we've been calling them, "astronaut crumbles."

Another friend works with one of those save-the-graywolf outfits, and he came up with one of the best food scams I've ever heard of. He's never been shy about calling customer service satisfaction lines and complaining that the product was faulty or had expired before the best-by date. Weeks in advance, he plans what he will eat, goes to the grocery store, and writes down phone numbers on packaged food he'd like in his cabinets. Then he calls to complain; coupons come by mail. The scam also works with dinners at chain restaurants—calling Red Lobster to criticize the service granted him free bounty of the sea.

I polled my friends once for the recipes they used the most often—the cheapest ingredients, the biggest stretch of the dollar. They responded with ramen soup, lentil soup, kidney beans dressed up a little in garlic, oats, and several varieties of canned tuna over pasta. I'm mostly living off of black beans and rice and, in the summer, fresh fruit.

I gather fruit from neighborhood trees. I have always

foraged around the house; I'm from the country. You could catch and boil tiny crawdads and minnows from the creek, steal pears from someone else's tree, and taste-test foliage and berries for edibility. I only got poisoned once, after dining on several apples that must have been a little funky, because I spent the next day suffering from dizziness and headaches. Still, I've gotten food poisoning more often from cheap restaurant food than from trees.

A neighborhood I lived in had so much food in the summer and fall that I drew a map detailing the locations of apples, apricots, blackberries, cherries, pears, plums, and raspberries so I wouldn't forget the following year. Other goodies grew in yards: chamomile, clover, dandelions, lavender, nasturtium, and rosemary. While I've never asked permission, I choose plants in abandoned lots or apartment complexes before venturing onto private property. Usually, it's sunny outside and there are people around, and when people see me picking fruit, they stop to join me.

Once I was at a plum tree in front of a complex, putting the fruit in a grocery bag. A blond couple came out from an apartment with a five-gallon bucket and asked if I knew how to make a plum pie. I recommended adding a touch of clove; I was planning on making spiced jam that I thought would go well with prosciutto and ciabatta. A middle-aged man pulled up, coming home from grocery shopping, and after unloading bags, he stopped to pick a few plums. Then a passing car filled with Mexican American gangsters screeched to a halt. The tattooed gangsters got out and the blond couple went inside. The *vatos* asked me about the tree and I answered their questions: no, I didn't live here or own the tree; yes, the plums are very juicy and sweet; yes, come try some with me. They ate some. The blond couple returned. Some teens sauntering down the sidewalk saw us all there and asked to have some plums. Soon almost a dozen people were around this one tree, everyone enjoying plums.

Such scenes never developed when I picked through a Dumpster behind a restaurant. I only went Dumpster diving a couple times, and I never went alone. Bakery trash was the best bet because bagels are baked fresh every morning and, if not sold that day, are thrown out. One can collect a month's worth of bagels with some—what I would like to believe was cinnamon—goo spilled on them.

Even though the food has become trash on its way to the landfill, to rot with defunct electronics, cat litter, decapitated Barbies, "organic" and inorganic goods, and even though young people in Portland were making it look hip, normalizing the behavior, rooting through a Dumpster for bagels still felt gross—desperation mixed with thievery. When imagining what I would say to a cop if one showed up behind the bagel joint, I never found the right words to practice, the best justification. I'd rather not have been seen; I never figured out how to "own" the act like those hipsters who invited me along. That's why it was preferable to go with someone else, a friend who's better at talking, or at least another set of eyes and ears.

After I graduated college, the recession had hit what we hoped would be its worst point, and the best job I could land was an unpaid, illegal internship with a children's theater nonprofit. Because during college I had only worked part-time, I did not qualify for unemployment benefits. For a while I ate whatever I could combine from foraging with what the food bank offered.

This food bank typically had the best food from Trader Joe's and Whole Foods, and vegetables ripe beyond comparison from the farmer's market. To get in, I simply had to stand outside in line for an hour, and on most visits, when it wasn't raining too hard, I brought a book of poetry from the library to pass the time. Others in line, either out of boredom or curiosity, would often ask about these books. They'd want to hear a poem. Reading over Li-Young Lee's "A Hymn to Childhood"—"Childhood? Which childhood? / The one that didn't last?"—I spoke with some elderly Asians about memory, longing, and racism in America while we waited for access to five pounds of frozen blueberries, a pound of lentils, and so much imitation crab that we would later wish we'd never laid eyes on the stuff.

When I was stuck, broke, and alone, I stayed with some homeless people in a tent city. I wish I could call it urban camping or some other euphemism, but the people were unpredictable and you could not see the stars. A Native American woman befriended me and, I believe, protected me. I think I reminded her of her teenage daughters whom she did not have rights to visit. She gave me a pallet to sleep on and some Oreos and Cheetos that were dropped off by some church group. She and I waited under a makeshift shelter with her flea-ridden puppy, waiting for a chain of social interactions to happen so I could use a cell to call a long-distance friend who could come help.

I've heard that we have programs in some public schools to teach children that food grows outside, not in fluorescent grocery store aisles, because our built environment disconnects us from our basic nature. But nature is more complicated than what is outside. It isn't just the plums growing on the tree; it's also adapting to the structures that control access to food, and succeeding in spite of them. Maturing in a recession means experiencing food scarcity, and we're still the same basic creatures we've been for millions of years, highly adaptable and sociable.

Recently, on the sidewalk outside the food bank, on a dreary morning, I stood next to an African American man who had a good spot under an awning and was doing something on his iPhone while we waited. I felt the cold down in my bones, and it was too wet to read poetry where I stood, so I asked him, "Are you checking in on Foursquare? Vying for a position as 'mayor'?"

He laughed and said, "Leaving a review of that stale bread I got last week."

We joked a little more and he let me stand under his awning, while he showed me an article on his phone. Later, perhaps, he would be cooking at home and posting photos of his dinner to Facebook or Instagram—inviting his friends to join him through their screens. Even if it's not as cozy as a Sunday night dinner, dining would still be an activity to rally around, display, and share.

As the rain picked up, I walked home through the city

streets with a frozen chicken, a pound of rice, and some bruised apples. A church bell rang through the elms, spring leafed out like a sphinx, and down the road I saw an apricot tree that will begin budding any day now.

To Love an Owl

Abby McBride

At the north end of Bog Road in Jackson, Maine, a line
of parked cars slowly lengthened along the dirty road-
side snowbank. Trunks were opened and gently slammed.
Tripods were unfolded, spotting scopes set up. Heavily
bundled people with binoculars and cameras crossed the
road and congregated at openings in the trees, speaking in
hushed, excited voices, peering through tangles of branches.

Don and I found a spot next to a big man in a camou-
flage jacket. The man was hunched over his camera, long
zoom lens trained on a distant tree. In that tree I could see
a lump, and that lump, I knew, must be a great gray owl.

Though our winter clothes helped conceal it, we were the
only twenty-somethings in this crowd of older birders. We
had been watching birds semiseriously for less than a year.
But I'd done my research, and I knew as well as anyone that
this owl of the far northern forests didn't belong in Maine.

With its imposing height and deceptively massive coat of feathers, the great gray owl dwarfs our biggest native owl, the great horned, though it actually weighs less. This bird was probably even lighter than it should have been. It would never have been this far outside of its range, or out in broad daylight, unless it was having trouble finding food.

When a local birder spotted the owl three days ago, he'd been faced with a decision. He could share the news with an online network of bird aficionados, who would trek from the far reaches of New England for the chance of a sighting. Or he could keep it to himself and leave the owl in peace. He had made his choice, and Don and I were among the dozens or hundreds of people who read his email on the regional birding email list. We'd been getting hooked on birding, this age-old pastime that was evolving its way into the digital social frenzy of the twenty-first century. The idea of a great gray owl, the promise of coming face to face with this winged creature from the boreal wilderness, had seemed too alluring to resist.

Now my binoculars were trained on the distant owl, though it was barely shifting on its perch and the view was blurred with out-of-focus branches. Come closer, I urged it silently, knowing better than to trespass for a better look. I watched and watched, ignoring my cold fingers and face.

All at once, the grayish form dropped from the bare branches, seeming to expand in flight. With slow and silent wing beats it swept low over a snow-covered clearing and toward someone's house, landing with a sway of needles in a lone pine tree. The watchers all picked up their scopes and hustled down the road after it, their efforts at subtlety fraying in the excitement. Maybe some of them had come just to check the species off of their life lists. Most, I felt sure, were wildlife lovers and conservationists, people who would savor this experience and share it with others through stories or blog posts or photo albums.

The camouflaged photographer ended up beside Don and me again, just at the end of the driveway. The enormous gray-brown bird was in full view now, and close. The camera shutter whirred.

From its perch the owl faced fixedly in one direction, its head cocked. A few minutes later its disk-shaped face rotated and settled on a new direction, a new angle. It was listening: listening for the scritching, rustling, foot-pattering of voles under the snow cover. Once, the owl leaned forward and smoothly glided down, down, splaying its wings to plow talons-first into the snow. I watched, holding my breath. But no rodent struggled in its talons, not this time. Were we distracting it? The owl launched itself back into the air, great wings laboring, and flew back to its tree.

While we stood watching, a woman came out of the house and approached our photographer friend. He was welcome to come closer to the pine tree, if he wanted, and would he send her a picture afterward? Don and I were beckoned in along with him, and we could hardly believe our luck. Gone was the official boundary between us and the owl. We made our way softly to the far end of the gravel driveway. We crept through deep snow to within a stone's throw of the pine.

Now I could see the owl in its full glory: cloud-gray and brown mottled feathers, black-and-white bow tie, keen yellow eyes. It turned its gaze toward me, seeming to stare for a full minute. Then it turned away.

After the two-hour drive home to Bar Harbor, we still felt the elation of our encounter with the owl. We looked forward to future birds and a future of birding. The photographer emailed us a beautiful shot of the owl in the pine tree, its wings spread wide. We hoped that it would catch a few voles, that it would find its way home by the end of the winter.

The owl could have moved on from Bog Road to another more remote spot in the deep Maine woods. It could have slipped right off the radar of the birding community, and we could have held onto our optimistic delusion. But the owl never left that rural backyard in Jackson. Two days later, we read on the email list that it had died, pitifully emaciated, the skin under its perfect-looking plumage riddled with parasites.

Birding didn't kill the owl and neither did we. But suddenly my supposed love of birds felt miserably selfish. Maybe we shouldn't have gone to Jackson, shouldn't have exploited that great gray owl's darkest hour. We could have stayed home and never entangled ourselves in the quiet little tragedy that played out in the woods that week. Then I wouldn't feel guilty, wouldn't feel pain for the plight of an owl.

I thought about it. I knew that I would keep worrying and wondering. I would keep on spending time with birds.

But I'll Still Be Here

James Orbesen

I'm a child of the 1990s, raised in a school district sensitive to the environment. Once, my class was loaded onto a school bus routed to the Lake County landfill. A guide pointed to the mountains of trash, crowned with seagulls, where garbage trucks trundled like gigantic green cockroaches among the mounds, and intoned: "This is from you." "Don't worry," the guide added, "here is the recycling center, where we take what's old and make it new again." We got to see where the garbage went, along with hearing long lectures on the meaning of numbers centered in the recyclable symbol.

My conservationist education started in places that smelled less than pleasant. It began when I visited the wetlands behind my elementary school, Cotton Creek, in Island Lake, Illinois. I trudged through muck in rubber boots, spotting herons and cranes among the cattails and tall grasses, told how valuable these endangered spaces were to the ecology of northeastern Illinois. The year was 1996, a relatively mild year for habitat destruction. I was in fourth grade. My whole class received paper workbooks emblazoned with a logo, an illustrated green tree frog not unlike that of the restaurant chain–cum–gift shop Rainforest Cafe, another '90s creation. The workbooks detailed, in fourth-grade terms, what the rain forest was, how quickly it was disappearing, and why it was so vital, the green lungs of Earth. I learned about conservation, biodiversity, where oxygen came from. "Slash-and-burn" and "exploitation" entered my vocabulary.

Environmental protection, as a movement, seemed to be on an upswing. Figures from the Brazilian National Institute for Space Research (INPE) indicated that a paltry 7,012 square miles of virgin forest fell beneath the lumberjack's axe in 1996. Progress? For a fourth-grader, certainly. Compared to the slaughter of 1995, when 11,220 square miles fell, it appeared our planet was on the mend.

Perhaps it had something to do with the songs we sang in class.

On top of the workbooks, lectures, videos, and even stuffed animals doled out in class, we sang songs about the rain forest. They were the standard VHS sing-alongs for youngsters, with lots of chorus and repetition and a bouncing ball for each song, jumping from lyric to lyric. I distinctly recall a cartoon jungle floating in the foreground during the sing-alongs, revealing rare and exotic animals hiding within. But the one song I remember most vividly was suitably descriptive of the entire classroom experience. The bass was rhythmic, soothing, vaguely primal. Tree frogs subbed in as an ersatz horn section. A khaki-clad human, a holdover from Ted Turner's *Captain Planet* perhaps, acted as tour guide/song coach.

I remember only one line:

"The tropical rain forest / It's the tropical rain forest / The tropical rain forest."

Stating the obvious to children would become a soul-searching endeavor once that youngling became an adult. I see that now. It's as if the lesson plan, itself, along with all the instructional materials, were still being worked out, instructors trying to figure themselves out. It was infinitely more complex than the multiplication tables and state capitals that typically filled class time. Students and teachers both stumbled in the brush, singing and coloring pictures of jaguars. Occasionally, I ate at a Rainforest Cafe, soaking in its animatronic animals. Because Rainforest Cafe's marketing stated a portion of its profits were donated to conservationist activities, and I recognized the parallel between the restaurant's mascot and the one from school, I felt part of something much larger, proactive, and powerful.

My childhood seemed a golden-hued era for environmental consciousness. *Captain Planet* ("The power is yours!") aired on Saturday mornings. I had all the plastic action figures, even a Captain Planet that turned colors in different water temperatures, indicating whether he was "cleansed" or "polluted." An entire multi-month educational unit in fourth grade, the moderate popularity of environmentally conscious cartoons, the seeding of endangered ecosystem-themed restaurants at area malls—all signaled that caring about the environment was a mainstream concern. I see these efforts, now, reinforce a common American attribute: if you want to champion a cause, slap a price tag on it.

Considering the false start of the Kyoto Protocol in the United States, maybe the 1990s weren't as golden-hued as I remembered. Just because something switches tracks, becomes mainstream, doesn't mean people take it fully seriously. As a fourth-grader, singing along with my classmates, coloring tree frogs like rainbows, I took my heightened awareness seriously, as seriously as a fourth-grader can take something. The impulse to be environmentally conscious stuck with me even as I advanced grades, farther and farther away from those initial lessons. Did I forget to recycle on occasion? Yes. Did I drive, rather than walk, to work? Yes. Did I even mostly forget the songs I'd sung? Yes. But what I think my childhood exposure to environmental awareness did was convince me that the adults were on the job. I was only nine or ten when the songs began. My trust in adult authority was wholly intact. I had a few years before the hormones kicked in. The grown-ups had it all covered. They had this environment thing fixed. I didn't learn about Kyoto until I was much older. I didn't put two and two together when my friends' parents started buying bigger and bigger vehicles. I never realized we learned about saving the rain forest from paper workbooks and plastic tchotchkes.

I trusted that older generations would have our best

interests in mind. I heard the chorus "The children are our future" often enough growing up. I bought it. Deforestation, pollution, species extinction, and global warming—it all would be taken care of. Why? Because I would still be here. I'd be around when all the Really Bad Things dropped, the dangers I learned about in fourth grade finally catching up. Why should my generation be left to clean up the mistakes of our parents and grandparents? Weren't children instructed, over and over, by their elders to pick up their toys and to clean their room? Those lessons came from some deep-seated impulse of taking responsibility for messes and spills.

Eventually, I caught on. These previous generations might have less at stake in this issue than their offspring. It was like ascending on escalator—I inevitably saw things from a different, broader perspective. An uncle once told me a story. His son, my older cousin, experienced a similar environmentally conscious classroom lesson but on a much smaller scale. The focus was on a particular bird, a species of endangered owl. The class learned about the threatened *Strigidae*, the odds they faced from increased human activity, and the students were encouraged to write a letter to their local congressperson, urging the protection of endangered species and the encouragement of responsible development. My uncle caught wind of this assignment, went to the school's principal, and complained. I'm not sure what happened to the letters written by the other students. Perhaps my uncle shut down the whole assignment with a threat of litigation. My cousin was exempted from the lesson and received a stay from advocating conservation.

When telling the story, my uncle smiled, puffing out his chest, saying he did it as a strike against environmentalists who wanted to take away American jobs. I was in my mid-teens. I hadn't yet realized the level of obstruction from those denying the impact of human activity on the environment. Most strikingly, I remember my uncle stating he wouldn't trade a single lumberjack for all the owls in America. I thought through my uncle's motivations, feeling as if my face had been rubbed into fresh snow, a whitewash, a hosing. I couldn't compute why anyone would be proud to *not* work toward preventing species extinction, to be proud of the diminishing biosphere. Perhaps the politicizing of the classroom bothered him. Perhaps he felt the teacher was pressing values onto his son. But what's harmful about wanting to conserve nature? Is that not a hallmark of being conservative, an ethos slathered heavily over my family? Was it such a problem that a teacher had encouraged students to become active, to develop their burgeoning voices, to fight for their birthright: a clean and living planet? I paid closer attention to the rhetoric many adults used to discuss the environment.

Many in power only cared about the environment to a certain point, this far and no further. I did all the work expected of me in fourth grade, assuming what I understood in the classroom mirrored what people believed on the outside. Instead, there was a line in the sand for adults and the environment. Protect it, yes. But what'll it cost me? I discovered Kyoto was rejected because no ceiling could be tolerated on economic growth. The logic struck me as similar to someone dismantling his house, selling the scrap to turn a buck. Would a rise in fuel prices—any rise—be tolerated if it protected the planet? Unlikely. What about a carbon tax to dial back an increase in global temperatures? That would kill jobs. How about the abandonment of familiar, extractive, destructive, dead-end industries in favor of cleaner, greener, less cost-effective, new ones? Beyond countenance. Let's frack and burn corn when the oil runs out. This manifested in my uncle, and in friends' parents who drove Escalades and Tahoes a few blocks for groceries through my suburban town. Habit, routine, and comfort often trumped the roles I assumed adults should play as custodians, caretakers, and educators. Bets were hedged on the consequences of environmental pillaging coming with a built-in delay. All the easier to kick the can down the road.

Fourth grade instilled in me an appreciation for the biosphere I otherwise wouldn't have come by until much later, if ever. Those songs and activities provided me an awareness of an ongoing problem, one urgently in need of a solution. However, that awareness made it much harder to reconcile what I learned in the classroom with what happens in practice. Considering the state of things and the even worse-off place this country is in now when it comes to climate issues, it isn't hard to fathom my disappointment, my early onset cynicism. It's had a hardening effect on me.

Now, at twenty-six, I can't shrug off the feeling that I,

along with all other former fourth-graders, have been bamboozled. Robert Costanza, former director of the Gund Institute for Ecological Economics at the University of Vermont, popularized the concept of "social traps," short-term behaviors that trump long-term goals. Human irrationality could, quite easily, result in spending $1.50 to take home $1, the result of "sunk costs." Items already owned and familiar are assigned undue value over those that are unfamiliar, even if the latter are demonstrably better. Sound familiar? I've increasingly felt bamboozled because younger people have been left with a mess that has supposedly been handled. Reality shows it certainly hasn't been.

Climatologists warn immediate action is required before temperatures rise beyond a manageable level. It is unlikely any timely action will be taken, though anything is possible. However, if circumstances are already so dire, we may already have a foot in the grave. There is an inherent delay in environmental consequences. The fossil fuels burned now don't throw their toxic weight around for several decades. My generation is just now reaching positions of power where influence can be directed. But it might be too late. We will still be here. We will have to suck up future Katrinas, Sandys, droughts, wildfires, and rising oceans while those who brought us to this point will be dead. Aside from a few brave voices—Bill McKibben or Al Gore to name two—we've been given a bad bill of goods. The deck is stacked against the young.

I don't regret anything I've learned, certainly not what I took away from fourth grade. Ignorance is what's placed us in this precarious space. But ignorance is bliss. That saying was never truer than it is today. Perhaps predictions are overblown and we'll lose nothing more valuable than a few green tree frogs. What are tree frogs in comparison to the genius of our creation: cars, action figures, chain restaurants? What are owls, after all? Simply things to be consumed, and consumed readily and heartily. The only regret I have is something our culture is obsessed with: youth. I regret the youth I possess and the longer life I'll lead to better see the wilting and eradication of the trees. Life itself will become exhaust spewed from the common tailpipe, or be turned into something consumable and marketable—Rainforest Cafe writ large against a *Blade Runner* backdrop.

My education has made it plainly clear: I'll still be here.

PART II.
THINKING LIKE A RIVER

An Orange County Almanac

Adventures in Suburban Ecology

Jason M. Brown

My nonstop flight from New York to LAX is arriving and the crackle-soft voice of the flight attendant shifts me in my window seat. Through the small pane of glass I can see my hometown of Yorba Linda creeping up the foothills of Orange County, indistinguishable from the rest of the Southern California megalopolis. My slow-fade window backdrop had started with eastern forests that melted into crop circles, then into meandering shades of desert tan. In short order, the tangle of north-south ridges that divide Southern California's coastal plain from its high desert gave way to the bedazzling microchip geometry of sprawling civilization. With the ocean on one side, mountains on the other, and sparkling humanity in between, the lines drawn dividing culture from nature were all too visible.

As a kid growing up in Orange County, nature was this

place we drove to. Each summer, my family would pack into the minivan for a whirlwind tour of Yellowstone, Yosemite, or Mount Whitney. Pristine places, pine-scented air, fishing, and long meandering hikes. In the cooler months we might camp among the Joshua trees of the high desert, but we were always *going* to nature. It didn't seem to bother us that subdivisions and mini-mansions steadily devoured the chaparral hillsides and historic orange and avocado groves of our once-sleepy corner of the county, so long as each summer we could flee to pristine places far from the smoggy, fast-paced life of the suburbs.

Our ancestors had supposedly reclaimed this desolate wilderness from the "idle savage" and hostile Mother Nature. In the good old days, Orange County was promoted as a Garden of Eden paradise, boasting mild temperatures, millions of acres of lush irrigated vegetable gardens, and fruit orchards surrounded by undulating hills of oak and sage. But after the post–World War II boom, the "Orange" in Orange County became just another hue on the planners' palette: pastel, pavement, repeat. Today, we certainly wouldn't use the word "natural" to describe Orange County, or assume that things like "ecology" have much to do with this sprawling empire. That's certainly how I felt when I left home as a twenty-something hoping to make a connection to nature through various back-to-the-land internships, graduate degrees, and backpacking treks.

I was certainly not alone in seeing the world this way; our modern civilization has inherited five hundred years or so of talking about the human domain—culture—as totally separate from just about everything else—nature. Look at any map of the world, and the defining boundaries are those between land and sea, countries, and most often around nature. The lines that mostly began in our heads, the ones we used to draw neat and tidy boundaries around ourselves and around nature, have become real in the way we construct our cities and live our lives. Southern California is full of these lines—not only between the United States and Mexico, but also between the myriad municipal, state, and national parks that embellish the coasts, wetlands, and mountains of the Golden State.

I have been reading a lot about these lines and boundaries we have drawn in the cultural sand; about how these lines and boundaries have hurt people, and places; and about how in an era of climate change, they might even be threatening our very existence. I am beginning to wonder if perhaps we should get rid of them, or at least redraw them. So each time I return to the County of Orange—for holidays, birthdays, births, backpacking trips with my brothers—the lines that seemed so clear to me growing up blur just a little bit more, and the differences between "us" and "them" slowly fade into thin air.

During my most recent trip, while strolling through the familiar streets of my childhood, I stumbled upon a cherished row of eucalyptus trees (*Eucalyptus globulus*) that lines a nearby street. A pickup truck's worth of workers were cleaning up after their morning task, and the soft consonants of Spanish bounced from mouths to ears. It appeared that they had just finished delimbing one of the eucalyptus trees, which stood stark and naked among its shaggy-clad companions. One of the workers prepared to make a final cut at the base of the trunk. As his chainsaw sputtered and choked, my mind began to wander in sync with the whine of metal teeth incising the fat, tan trunk. I passed by these trees almost daily growing up and never really put them into any kind of historical or ecological context. I had recently been reading about the natural history of Orange County, and though I knew these trees were old, it now made sense that they had no doubt been planted to protect orange groves that had once covered the county against the Santa Ana winds.

I watched as the first few inches of the saw's sweep transected the tree's outer bark and newest growth rings. The tree rustled and I imagined the blade cutting through the growth rings that correspond to my thirty-something years of life on this earth. It would pass by rings made during my time in graduate school and college, the two years spent as a Mormon missionary in the Dominican Republic, high school, my first kiss, first camping trip, and my birth.

One by one, the rest of the crew stopped their tasks and began watching the tree for signs of tilt as the blade continued past growth rings made in the 1970s, when the orange and avocado groves the eucalyptus protected were being swallowed whole by subdivisions and strip malls (my parents' home was built during this time). As the blade cut deeper, and the tree's once-flesh-now-dust flew into the air, it passed the 1960s—Nixon, hippies; 1950s—Cold War; 1940s—WWII; 1930s—depressions, dust bowls; and 1920s—prohibition and revivals. Buried deep inside the bole of the tree, the blade approached the growth rings of 1913, the year the first avocado trees were planted, and the year Richard Nixon was born, just down the street from where I stood.

Finally, the sawyer cut through the teetering eucalyptus's infant growth rings, which must have been laid around 1910, when the Janss Investment Company purchased a portion of the Rancho Cañon de Santa Ana and began subdividing it into ten- and twenty-acre agricultural parcels which would later become Yorba Linda.

With a snap and a crack the truncated bole thudded to the path along the sidewalk and the sawyer quickly began to buck it into manageable sections. One of the other workers directed the few backed-up cars to pass, and as I walked past the downed eucalyptus and crew, I caught the tail end of a scowl cast by an older woman in a black Mercedes as she surveyed the scene and sped off. For many in California, illegal immigration is a touchy subject. Perhaps she was sizing up the tan-skinned workers as possible suspects—lines and boundaries.

Like the Europeans, Mexicans, Chinese, and other ethnicities that call California home, eucalyptus trees are immigrants. Native to Australia, they were brought to California during the gold rush of 1849 with one of the thousands of Australians who left Sydney hoping to strike it rich. And like the immigrants they accompanied, the eucalyptus found fertile soil and a favorable climate in the California coastal sage and prairies. For a few years thereafter the eucalyptus was officially promoted as a "wonder tree" that would save California from an impending timber famine and whose pungent leaves were reputed to have medicinal properties. Many soon realized, however, that the structural properties that gave eucalyptus its reputation as a good timber tree had come from the wood of centuries-old groves in southern Australia. The wood of the fast-growing young trees, saturated with water, warped and cracked when harvested in California and was therefore useless. Although commercial production came to an abrupt halt, the tree naturalized itself throughout the coastal region of central and southern California.

Eucalyptus has since become such an iconic part of California's scenic heritage that there is an entire landscape painting genre named after it. However, in an age of ecological correctness, the eucalypts have become easy targets for those who are trying to restore nature to some semblance of what it once was before we came along and bulldozed everything in the name of culture.

One way of restoring ecological integrity is to get rid of plants and animals that did not evolve in a given ecosystem, the plants and animals most often called nonnative, exotic, or alien species. These plants were either brought here intentionally or hitched a ride with us. However, despite the hundreds of nonnative species that have naturalized since the European colonization of the Americas, in California the eucalyptus has been singled out as a symbol of a gaggle of ecological menaces known as "invasive" species. In his 2002 article "America's Largest Weed," ecologist Ted Williams calls for the total removal of eucalypts or, as he refers to them, "eucs." For restorationists like Williams, eucalypts simply do not belong in California, despite their ability to adapt to our climate.

California ecologists have in many cases removed eucalypts from public lands in order to restore native chaparral and coastal ecosystems, though hundreds of other nonnative plants remain in these parks. In the Channel Islands National Park, just off the coast of Southern California, officials have decided to keep some eucalypts that are close to historic structures as part of the *cultural* heritage of the parks, while removing them from other parts of the island.

As I continued my walk toward the mesquite hills above my parents' subdivision, it struck me that the language used to talk about eucalypts as an ecological menace and the language used to ostracize illegal immigrants as social pariahs is similar. Both discourses make use of epithets—"eucs" or "wetbacks"—to distance and demonize. Both eucalypts and immigrants are often derided for uncontrolled reproduction and the danger they pose to native ways of life, whether that be biological competition for growing space or economic competition for jobs. In a strange twist the eucalypts are anthropomorphized in order to be dehumanized, and illegal immigrants are dehumanized in order to be denaturalized. Lines and boundaries.

Ironically, the debate over removal of eucalyptus trees from spaces delineated as "natural" exposes how drawing a stark boundary between culture and nature is not so easily accomplished. Those who love the eucalyptus accuse folks like Ted Williams of ecological purism, or of engaging in a kind of arboreal "ethnic" cleansing in the name of native floral supremacy. Williams and others have argued that protecting native species is, in the end, about protecting global biodiversity in the face of the supposed homogenizing effect of invasive exotic species like eucalyptus.

However, as Emma Marris shows in her book *Rambunctious Garden*, global extinction caused by invasive species is relatively rare, especially by relatively benign exotics like eucalyptus. Extinction from invasive species is mostly happening on small islands such as Guam, where the brown tree snake, introduced to Guam after World War II, has decimated bird populations. Eucalyptus trees have not caused the extinction of a single species; while the trees have had a negative impact on some birds whose beaks are sealed shut by eucalyptus sap, they also provide critical winter habitat to migrating monarch butterflies and other native species that have now adapted to them.

Certainly my ancestors were once immigrants. And certainly all native plants on the Channel Islands arrived in succession. So, if eucalypts have adapted to California, and are not causing widespread extinction, why should we spend precious resources to remove them? Lines and boundaries.

I am not saying that all human activity is benign; it is not. We must undo the damage we have inflicted onto this planet. Nor am I advocating for an abandonment of the protected-area franchise, which has protected millions of species from our lust for money and power. But what both the Channel Islands case and the woman in the black Mercedes say to me is just how deeply ingrained the boundaries we draw around the other can become—between culture and culture, *and* between culture and nature. It is time to rethink these lines and boundaries.

As I sit in the airport terminal waiting for my return flight to the East Coast, I notice a small house sparrow dip and weave through the airport corridors. Even in a world where we have laid an iron curtain between culture and nature, there are always cracks where the two bleed together. The domains of culture and nature don't exist independently. Even a place as developed and overrun by *Homo sapiens sapiens* as Southern California shares something of the infinite complexity that emerges between these cracks. The good— if sometimes scary—news is that the cracks are getting bigger.

The moral to the story is not that one can *find* "nature" in Orange County if one would just look hard enough; nor is it that intact, robust ecosystems are not important, or that they are wholly social constructions. But in a world of increasing ecological catastrophe, the solution is not necessarily to ramp up our technological strength over a more aggressive "nature"; nor is it necessarily to bring back pristine ecologies by removing every last scrap of nonnative species.

This is because ecology is not a place—it is not a thing we have control over; ecology is the space *between* things, including us. Believing that there are natural places and natural things, and totally separate cultural places and cultural things, denies the inherent beauty, creativity, agency, and interdependence of all things, even eucalypts and immigrants. Climate change doesn't care whether our parks look the same as they did two hundred years ago, and human compassion does not respect borders between nations.

There are no easy answers moving forward; surely we must do something different if we are to survive as a species. But rather than continuing to police the boundaries between ourselves and the other, perhaps the task ahead is to dismantle the boundaries we have constructed between ourselves and everything else and to watch what happens.

Other, Wise

Cameron Conaway

The megalopolis madness of Bangkok doesn't so much sprawl as flail everywhere you'll ever and never need to be. There's the pulse of fluorescent advertisements, fluorescent taxis, and fluorescent high-heels and the black jumble of electrical wires crammed into lopsided balls, duct-taped, then draped near intersections. The pulse is a microcosm for the artifice of modernity: build it up, make it shine, all will be fine.

We were twenty-five years old, my then-fiancée Maggie and I, and for years we'd been hell-bent on achieving things as you're supposed to. We even had a wall-sized poster that read "Let No One Outwork You Today!"

Ten-hour workdays in Charlottesville, Virginia, became twelve, then thirteen. Burnout and breakdown always felt around the corner. So in early 2010 when we were at a Thai restaurant it was at once surprising and entirely expected when I saw Maggie's smile slowly expand and her eyes fill with tears.

"I know what I need, babe," she said. "I need to live abroad. I want to teach abroad."

With that she broke eye contact with me, looked around at the Buddha figurines and the faux-marble elephant statues, and then steadied her eyes back on mine:

"Thailand?"

Jon Kabat-Zinn, professor emeritus and creator of Mindfulness-Based Stress Reduction at UMass Medical School, often says, "When you are in the shower, check to see if you are really in the shower." His point is that so often we move through life without being truly present where we are. Maggie and I were not where we were. Charlottesville was our physical environment, but the connection ended there. The weight of our work had separated us from place, a place we intentionally moved to because we loved its sense of community—a community that took seriously the arts, education, and issues of social and environmental justice. We wanted to be there in the Kabat-Zinn sense, and we thought this would eventually come with a simple formula: focus on a passion + "Let No One Outwork You Today!"

We lived the formula so hard it failed us, though it worked brilliantly to separate us from our connections back home in Pennsylvania, to create tension in our own rela-

tionship, to distance us from Charlottesville, and to starve
the seed of resistance within us—a seed that felt inequality
in America but believed it could be crushed when work and
ethic were given equal weight.

That night we researched and took notes, and the same
could be said for the nights of the next few months. Once
we were sure of the move and of Thailand, then the selling
began. Our DVDs, my car, her mattress—it all had to go
for us to afford this. We first met our customers on eBay
and Craigslist and then made the sales in the parking lot at
Shenandoah Joe coffee shop. The buyers were the typical
swindlers, but for the most part everything went smoothly.
Sometimes too smoothly. Criminally smoothly. Like when
I sold my lamp.

I stood in a strip mall parking lot and the transaction
was made entirely without the customers getting out of or
even stopping their car. They cruised slowly by, lowered the
passenger window, handed me the cash, and I handed them
the goods. Up went the window and off they went. No
words exchanged.

But each item we got rid of, and we didn't have many,
gave something back. Because we were working together as
a team, our own relationship began to deepen. This deep-
ening illuminated our other disconnections—to friends
back in Pennsylvania, to our environment here—and we,
often without realizing it, began shoring up those relationships. Surface conversations on Facebook instead became
more personal phone calls, hearing about new places to
hike became actual hikes, and our humdrum meals became

experiments with international recipes or exploring interesting restaurants in the area.

One year later and we're in Bangkok, the city whose real
name is the longest place-name in the world. Our first
days were about absorbing the shock factor of new—the
smell of raw fish and sharp spice upon waking, the reliance
on orange-vested motorcycle taxis to get around congested
traffic, automobile exhaust, and a language of seemingly
infinite vowel sounds that swirled in thick, sticky-rice air. It
was uncomfortable in good ways.

Here we were in the muddled middle of what we could
control and what we couldn't. We were here, really in the
shower of a place, uprooted, disconnected, and primed for
other ways of being and of being wise.

Primed for when the humble owner of a street-food stall
on Sukhumvit 50 exited the market with a full tray of raw
chicken meat, made it nearly all the way across the highway,
and then lost her balance after stepping into a pothole;
primed for when the chicken went flying through the air,
landed in the oil and sewage froth along the curb, and then
was run over by an onslaught of motorbikes; primed for
now having the distance to look back into the contours of
our lives to observe the screaming, curse-word-ridden action
we've been taught to embrace in such difficult moments;
primed for when she stood along the curb as a day's salary
was decimated before her eyes; and primed for when she
then looked to her stall mates, smiled, and said, *"Mai pen rai."*

Translation: No problem. Things will be okay.

They smiled back to her, offered countless mai pen rais, and pitched in to give her some of the chicken from their stall.

This moment was our outlet, a lived experience that plugged us back in to the environment around us and our place within it.

Lesson: You need not travel to travel. Other ways of being and of being wise are everywhere if you're primed to receive them.

One year later and this concrete Legoland built atop swamplands had become more natural to us than Canoe Creek State Park or any of Pennsylvania's other forested lands.

But I'd studied peak oil and carbon footprints in grad school.

But I'm a lifetime member of the Association for the Study of Literature and Environment.

No matter.

I now knew these lopsided sidewalks better than what memory, that rhythmic specter, gave me of the woods and snows and roads where I was born. Where I was and how primed I was to be in the shower of a place shaped my sense of home more than how long I lived somewhere else. Home, thanks in part to Skype and other gap-bridging technology, became more about the fluidity with which I could move in my environment, about what I could contribute to and receive from that environment, and about whether I shared this space—no matter how cramped or vast—with the person I loved.

• • •

Growing up, I noticed that progress was tied to making the natural world unnatural but more comfortable. Instead of riding a bike through a park we now had the option of riding a bike in the safety of a gym and with a TV screen that showed, in real time, a local park in our area. Television shows about the fascinating qualities of animals were steadily replaced with shows either about wrangling those animals or about how we've wiped them out and now must save the survivors.

Though I noticed this, I didn't understand it deeply until I was studying with environmental writers at Penn State Altoona and learned how the words "civilization" and "development" have typically been wielded like badges of honor. The terms often meant, at their core, that a collected group of people had created the greatest distance between themselves and the natural world, and that this was an achievement to be praised. They meant that this group of people had constructed their own environment inside an already-existing natural environment. The more layers between the former and the latter, it seemed, the more developed. The more layers between the haves and the have-nots, it seemed, the more developed.

These ideas were nurtured as I studied with other environmental writers while in graduate school at the University of Arizona. I'd think daily about how in order to feel at home and in my environment I needed to live off the grid somewhere in New Mexico (I had a particular community mapped out) rather than contributing to what I saw as the mess into which I had been born. But upon graduation I stayed with the mess, because love was there. In Charlottesville, I grew love and buried environmental grief.

But Bangkok brought that grief roaring back. It pulsed in the billboard that described the "coming soon" hotel being built where there once was a river as "beautiful," in how I'd take the skytrain to a skyscraper and then take an elevator or escalator to one of the top floors, where I'd run on a treadmill. It pulsed in the perfect auto-tuned voice pumping out of the speakers, and in the lobby piano keys that indented themselves to play Sergei Rachmaninoff's Piano Concerto no. 2.

Last week I saw a man here pass out on the skytrain. We were all packed in so tight he couldn't fall but went unconscious while standing against us. We were all plugged in— all fiddling, pinching, swiping, and scrolling on some interface in our face. I don't know how long he was out, but I got a hand on him before he started to fall into the gap created when a few people exited the train. When he came to, he said he was diabetic, and we got him some sugar.

What is it to be in touch with thousands on Twitter but not with those whose breath we can feel? How can our connected generation disconnect so we can connect? We've built it up, and we're making it shine, but I'm not sure all will be fine.

Tamale Traditions

*Cultivating an Understanding of Humans
and Non-human Nature through Food*

Amy Coplen

Clouds of corn flour rise as electric mixers whir the yellow masa. I brave the storm, leaning in to pour beef broth and red chile into the dough, and emerge covered in a fresh dusting of corn flour. No time to brush it off—I need to keep up with my mom and my grandma, who are quickly spreading finished masa onto corn husks, plopping down spoonfuls of shredded pork marinated in red chile, then wrapping and folding the husks around the mixture to form little steam jackets. My ten-year-old cousin giggles as I dodge the wet ingredients that are now sloshing around in and out of the mixing bowls. Her task is to tie up the tamales so they stay snugly wrapped while my auntie steams them in one of the three pots whistling on the stove. The kitchen cacophony drowns out the holiday music humming from the stereo, but no one seems to mind. I glance over my shoulder to take note of how quickly the masa is being used up and notice smears of yellow corn paste on my mom's nose and forehead. I grab a clean towel and wipe masa from her face and we burst into laughter. We've made an enormous mess! When the hysterics subside, we get back to work. It's half past four and we need to keep moving. Our goal is twenty-seven dozen tamales, one more than last year, and we won't settle for less.

I was born in the desert Southwest, where rich food traditions, including the communal preparation and consumption of tamales, chile rellenos, posole, and more, are passed from one generation to the next in kitchens just like mine. These kitchen customs are sustained by parallel traditions that thrive on the region's farmlands, some of which have been cultivated for more than four hundred years. Farmers preserve countless heirloom varieties, including spicy and acidic Chimayo chiles, nutty blue corn posole, and deep red and white speckled Anasazi beans. They grow these crops in landscapes shaped by centuries of careful stewarding, with water flowing through common property ditches, or acequias, dug by their ancestors more than four hundred years ago. Water serves as the lifeblood of acequia farmers and those who are sustained by the culturally significant foods they produce. This includes me, but as a child, I had no idea.

I was born in Belen, New Mexico, and so was my father. He grew up in a subdivision called Mariposa Park. Its houses were built in the early 1950s for returning World War II veterans, which included my grandfather, Papa

Frank. Curiously, a handful of acequias wound their way through the subdivision. Relics of a farming past, the acequias reminded Mariposa Park residents that the landscape was changing. Old farmland was making way for new development.

One acequia happened to sit just beyond my father's back fence. In the sweltering summers, he, his brothers and sister, and a band of neighborhood kids would seek relief, splashing around in the cool waters of the acequia. Each spring, they picked wild asparagus on its banks. Rumor had it that the Gerardi family imported asparagus seeds from Italy and that they had somehow been set loose, washing downstream and sowing themselves along the banks of the acequias. After the kids gathered the crisp green spears, my grandmother would sauté the harvest with a little butter and lemon juice. My father claims he hasn't tasted better asparagus since.

My childhood home was six miles and thirty years from his in the subdivision of Rio Communities, but the name isn't quite indicative of the experience. Asphalt and yellowish lawns served as the playground for the kids in my neighborhood.

After high school, I left for greener pastures to attend the University of New Mexico, an hour north in Albuquerque. There I learned the disturbing details of society's destruction of the environment and how climate change was threatening the lives and livelihoods of many communities, including my birthplace. While the Rio Grande valley where I grew up peers into a future of insufferable drought,

Gulf cities downstream face impending inundation by rising coastal waters. Poor nations, who have relatively little to do with causing global warming, will suffer its most severe consequences. And as we walk this fine line between unsettling weather anomalies and climate disaster, deniers mount misinformation campaigns against the scientific data pointing irrefutably to anthropogenic global warming. In the southwestern United States, and regions worldwide, farmer livelihoods, local food security, and community health are integrally linked to precious and limited water resources, and development and climate change threaten these relationships.

During college, when I drove south to visit my family and friends I couldn't help but see the irony of those sickly lawns contrasted by the desert landscape that stretches just beyond the border of Rio Communities. Six miles away, my father's childhood home went up for sale. He and his brothers and sister were overwhelmed with curiosity. How had it changed? What state was it in? What memories might a visit stir? My uncle, a newly licensed real estate agent, suggested a tour. My dad invited me to come along, and I gladly joined. As a kid, I hadn't been interested in his old asparagus and acequia stories, but as an adult with a budding understanding of human–nature relationships, I paid closer attention. I had the opportunity to see the landscape of my father's birthplace.

We opened the creaky door and were met by a musty smell. Quiet voices echoed with a certain hesitance at first, but soon inquiries of "Remember when?" and roars of "Take a look at this!" grew louder as old memories were revisited. I tried to be patient, but at first chance I made a beeline for the back door. I wanted to lay my eyes on that acequia.

My father followed me outside and we headed toward the back fence. We peered over to find that my father's childhood acequia had been filled in. In fact, there was no trace of the neighborhood's former network of irrigation canals. Over time, development had transformed an ancient agricultural landscape into an aging subdivision with parched dirt and yellow lawns. This was not the setting of my father's childhood, but one that more closely resembled my own. I mourned the transformation of a landscape that I knew only through stories. Never had humans and nature stood so diametrically opposed in my mind. Not only are we disconnected from the natural world, I thought, we are actively destroying it.

Since this visit to my father's childhood home, I've spent much time reflecting on my antagonistic view of humans and nature. In particular, I've come to understand the ways in which it limited me from examining the root causes of environmental degradation.

The human/nature dichotomy pervades our culture and mediates our daily lives. We are distant from the capitalist production practices that transform nature to meet our needs. We turn a knob and our homes are cooled or heated, while carbon dioxide warms our climate, causing desertification and inundation simultaneously in different parts of the world. We choose from a uniform selection of glossy tomatoes in the dead of winter, yet migrant farmworkers toil in slave-like conditions in Mexico and even in Florida. We text friends with our new smartphones, yet few of us are aware of the bloody conflict over mining of the electronic component coltan in the Democratic Republic of the Congo. Our physical distance from production processes enables us to ignore the social, political, and economic causes of environmental degradation. But, like it or not, these production practices constitute our relationship with nature and with one another. Nature is not a wilderness "out there." Nature is embedded in everything we do. Nature is us, and we are nature.

In his essay "The Trouble with Wilderness; or, Getting Back to the Wrong Nature," insightful environmental historian William Cronon argues that the concept of wilderness—a cultural construction defined by the absence of humans—"reproduce[s] the dualism that sets humanity and nature at opposite poles." Rather than work to repair the damage we've done to this earth, to rebuild a relationship between the human and nonhuman world, this dichotomy reinforces an idea of separateness, and a naïve notion that if we "leave it alone" nature will flourish.

But what about those who make their living by working the land? What about acequia farmers who understand the intricacies of nature better than any backpacker who might venture into the "wilderness" of a national forest? What about those who respectfully labor on the land to provide for us, both bodily and culturally? Using wilderness as a measure of our sustainability ignores our dependence on the land. It ignores the fact that high-density cities and the wilderness they make possible rely on resources extracted from the hinterlands, including farmlands that now extend globally. The human/nature dichotomy disregards the four-hundred-year legacy of ecologically beneficial acequia agriculture in the Southwest. It ignores the relationship between the farmer, the water, the land, and the gift of this corn masa forming in my mixing bowls—the corn masa that nourishes the body, the family, and cultural traditions.

When I head back to Oregon in a few days I will bring a piece of New Mexico with me via three dozen carefully assembled tamales, each one touched by the hands of my grandmother, my auntie, my cousin, and my mom. I've zigzagged the country over the past three years working to educate myself and to develop a better understanding of humanity's place, and my own place, in this world.

I put down roots in New Haven, Connecticut, using community gardens as a gateway to connect with and become a part of my new community. I captured the compelling stories of community gardeners who work the soil in a postindustrial landscape that has been classified as a food desert. Amid a dearth of supermarkets, rising unemployment, and increasing income disparity, these gardeners create a kind of shared community wealth; they contribute to food security, a vibrant urban ecology, and a strengthened sense of place. They taught me that no matter where we roam, as long as we can connect with food, we can connect with place, and we can connect with one another.

I moved back to New Mexico last summer to help teach a "foodshed field school" at my alma mater. We toured the farms and fields of New Mexico, interviewing farmers who provide us with our beans, green chile, and corn. We spent time cooking and eating together, learning traditional New Mexican recipes so that we might teach a new generation to make posole, rellenos, and—you guessed it—tamales.

Having settled in Portland, Oregon, a few months ago, a beautiful city well known for its access to pristine "wilderness," and 1,358 miles away from my family and my birthplace, I'm reminded of our inherent need for community. By community, I mean a sense of place, a bond with people, and a connection to nature. I believe we cannot have one without the other, for we make up our place. We are nature.

I'm building a new home here in the Northwest. I'm hiking in the Cascades, joining a nearby community garden, and appreciating the wet climate after spending most of my life in the desert. I've learned that the Yakama Indians consider salmon sacred and have been harvesting huckleberries in the region for millennia. With each bite of these important cultural foods I am connected to the waters of the White Salmon River and to the soil of Mount Adams. These experiences will help me cultivate a new sense of place here in the Northwest, where, as in many other places, food traditions prove that without nature there are no humans and without humans there is no nature.

Wherever my pursuit of knowledge takes me, I promise to return to the Southwest every December to continue my family's tamale tradition. We surpassed our goal of twenty-seven dozen, in case you were wondering. Including the three dozen that we ate that day, we made forty-two dozen tamales. One day I hope to add more hands to the tamale-making. When I bring my own children into this world, they will learn the food traditions that are so important to my family, and in doing so, they will not see themselves as separate from nature. They will learn at a young age that there is no distinction between a community of people and the earth that feeds them. And this understanding will empower them to be good stewards of the environment.

Wilderness of Blackberries

Craig A. Maier

I give thanks for the hours I have sought, studied, and volunteered in the wilderness of the western United States. At the same time, when I have been asked by professor, friend, or skeptic about the definition and value of wildness and wilderness, I have tended to grant the Midwest's disturbance-loving vine—the eastern black raspberry (*Rubus occidentalis*)—considerable standing.

I am not biased by fruit and flavor. I have savored the prickly pear cactus fruit in the high deserts while away on dusty backpacking treks, and I have also paused from stream surveys to supplement my lunch with salmonberries growing along streams draining the Siskiyou and the Cascade Crest. I will even admit that the thimbleberry that grows in the dusty shade of ponderosa in the Blue Mountain backcountry may pack a brighter flavor, but my favorite wild fruit remains the eastern blackberry.

Recently, one prodigious clump of stems staked claim in our Wisconsin yard, finding its niche in a hollow at the base of a large, decomposing stump. The seminal cane escaped early detection, and I have since declared this shrubby wonder off-limits to push mowers, weed whackers, and gloved defenders of lawn and order. Earlier this week, as I greedily devoured handfuls of sumptuous berries, their flavor jolted me back into one of my wildest adolescent experiences.

I grew up in the 1980s and '90s in a little house on six exurban acres—the lone developed lot of a subdivided farm field—left behind almost every day by two blue-collar parents. In our post–family farm landscape, plenty of infertile fields had been abandoned. The one next door was quickly growing up into ragweed, goldenrod, wild strawberry, feral oaks, brambles, prickly ash, and federally subsidized pine trees, planted quickly into rows across the sand, and later thinned by drought. The surrounding land was less and less amenable to the growing machinery of farming, and the community's affection for this glacial landscape had dwindled to near zero by the time I was old enough to comprehend that there were some places, other places, where people proclaimed their surroundings were beautiful.

Yet among the patches of weeds and young trees that surrounded us, there were whip-poor-wills and bobwhite quail—species that make birding by ear possible—and birds I've learned are now vanishingly rare in southern Wisconsin. Flocks of sandhill cranes nested in undrained wetlands and plied the farm fields for bugs and seeds. They, too, could not be ignored, as they were prone to rattling our summer mornings with their braying and croaking. Dad was not a scholar or an environmentalist, but he assured me that these raucous and wary creatures were no mere birds, but a link to the prehistory of Wisconsin. He related how the history of their tribe extended back toward the time of the dinosaurs, yet they had narrowly survived extinction in the era of my grandmother's childhood. Most mysterious, and subtle, was the flight of nighthawks through our summer evenings. These swept-wing birds swooped down, inverse parabolas to mirror the arc of a football passing inexpertly from my hand to my father's. Venus was there, too, bright evening star trailing after the sunset, another inhabitant of summer evenings in my Arcadia.

I was barely half a generation separated from a family lifestyle that had more to do with farming, fishing, and hunting than working in an office. At first we kept a few cows, and then sheep. One fall evening, when I was about three or four, my parents and brothers built the woven wire fence that defined our sheep pasture. As Dad tamped clay around a wooden fence post, he stopped and looked up, and I followed his gaze. A flock of Canada geese flew overhead, low enough for us to see the strain in their necks and individual feathers as they slowly pulled themselves forward through the sky in an aerial breaststroke. I listened intently to the whisper of their wings, as the vortex they left in their wake rippled overhead.

Considering my vivid memory of the moment, this passage of the wild geese was perhaps a formative event. In elementary school, I brought home countless books that illustrated and discussed the key taxa of America, such as the Blackbird, Warthog, and Fighting Falcon. In the family Helicopterae, I could readily distinguish between the AH-64 Apache and the more primitive AH-1, as well as the UH-60 Blackhawk and its Vietnam-era predecessor, the UH-1 "Huey." I also had a good eye for the nuances of various missiles of the U.S. armory, and found it odd that others had trouble telling apart the Maverick, Hellfire, Sidewinder, and Tomahawk. It was my first hint of the kind of passion that a restoration ecologist brings to distinguishing a centuries-old bur oak (*Quercus macrocarpa*) from a generic "tree," and to observing and identifying the blossoming flora, fruiting fungi, crawling and hopping invertebrates, and nesting birds one would expect to see under or within its boughs, bark, and spreading roots.

In that time, it was easy to forget the subtleties of the music of passing geese. My attention was captured by the Doppler scream of attack machines (an A-10, this machine) flying fast and low over our country school and the surrounding hills and farm fields. I was quite proud that our landscape and livelihoods could stand in for the West German farm and woodlot countryside that the tank-killing pilots would defend when the Warsaw Bloc armies started rolling across the Iron Curtain—or, if not proud, suitably alert to the forces at work, thanks to reading military history books rather than natural history books. Perhaps as a young, insatiable reader I had internalized what geopolitical forces like a policy of M.A.D. really meant, for life in Arcadia and on earth in general. Why care about a homeland when assured its only defense is mutually assured thermonuclear destruction of self and other?

My dutiful father continued to try to steer my attention back toward the land. But animal husbandry was not my chosen path. I ended my stint as shepherd and 4-H'er by high school, where academic objectives gave me the easy excuse of needing to focus on my studies instead. This was a welcome cover to avoid expressing my disinterest in rearing sheep, which meant dealing with all of the needs and idiosyncrasies of these semi-wild creatures. Moreover, I was no longer patient with 4-H procedures, which meant monthly meetings conducted under Robert's Rules of Order and completing annual record books.

Another tack of Dad's was berry picking. I was an unlikely sight—an adolescent pinned beneath a long-sleeved flannel shirt despite the insufferable July heat index, with an ungainly, absurd berry-carrying jug hung from my waist. Ever resourceful (a character trait bound to embarrass adolescents steeped in the throwaway values of the MAD era), Dad did not buy some kind of modern berry-handling device but made do with washing up a one-gallon plastic milk jug and cutting off its top. Worse yet, he showed me how to run a piece of baling twine through my belt loop and tie it around the jug handle. Nor did we set out by car to a paradise of lush berry bushes at a "pick your own" farm. Instead, I followed him into one of the disturbed habitats common to a rural landscape where crop acreage peaked somewhere around 1929. You may find such places wherever an old gully, rock pile, fencerow, or property line was ignored or forgotten. This is where you will find the expression of a reclamation program guided not by the Soil Conservation Service, U.S. Forest Service, Civilian Conservation Corps, or Riley Game Cooperative, but by whatever seeds cared to sprout and fight for sunlight and other resources on that patch of eroded subsoil.

Following Dad's lead, I ducked beneath rows of leaning box elders, threaded deer trails through nettle patches, and tested my balance against piles of fieldstone resting at their angle of repose. Despite those obstacles and the ensuing rush of sweat and bugs (enough to drench any bandanna and sting my eyes, and more than enough to yield an array of bites and welts to reproduce the entire pantheon of Greek constellations in red lumps), I was outside.

My motivation for enduring the lowly work, physical pain, and worse—potential embarrassment—was clear, or I might never have agreed to venture out initially, or, later, lobbied my father to do so. Though it might be chalked up to filial piety, self-medication (could early-1990s preteens diagnose Nature Deficit Disorder and prescribe time outdoors long before doctors caught on?), or love of fresh blackberries, the best of which I found stained my lips soon after I felt their plumpness on my fingers, these motivations were but moths dancing around the porch light: at the end of these labors was blackberry cobbler. The following day's dessert was often that luscious mix of sugar and berries topped with hearty homemade shortcakes.

It was not the plight of the rain forest (tropical or temperate), or America's Red Rock Wilderness Act, or the frightful scarcity of my own tallgrass prairie–oak savanna– wetland ecosystem that led me away from books and television. I experienced no teenage initiation into wild animal hunting. Instead, I began down the path toward a delight in wildness and wild places in search of the dark, sugary complexity of the eastern black raspberry—trading the Cold War dystopia of my books and early-onset Nature Deficit Disorder for a productive venture and adventure close at hand.

Since then, I have never found the indescribable taste of a real blackberry in fruit purchased at the store or at the farmer's market, or even grown out in the garden. Our backyard bush comes close in flavor, but it is really too convenient. To find a good blackberry, a wilder blackberry, one must follow the old fencerows and rock piles. The pattern I was given to follow suggests that one look for places where black cherries, elms, mulberries, and oaks have grown up near a field or farm road's opening, yet beyond the easy reach of plow, cow, herbicide drift, and bulldozer. That is where the blackbirds, thrashers, and towhees shit the seeds out in profusion, where the soil is untrodden, and where the profligate sunlight is filtered and softened by the screen of neighboring trees. It is where modern work, or modern gadgetry, is replaced for a time by an older rhythm of following and gathering. In such unlikely tangles of history, ecology, and family, I was primed to seek more of wild Wisconsin, and wild America, wherever I could find it. In such tangles I found an unmatched sweetness.

My Present Is Not Your Tombstone

Love and Loss in Utah's Canyon Country

Lauren McCrady

"Most of what I write about in this book is already gone
or going under fast. This is not a travel guide but an elegy.
A memorial. You're holding a tombstone in your hands."
EDWARD ABBEY, *Desert Solitaire*

"Those of us who live here know the heartbreak of loss."
TERRY TEMPEST WILLIAMS, *Red*

"A playground for the hip and idle, Moab seems like a town
designed by *Outside* magazine, shamelessly advocating the outdoors
as a playground and portraying nature as a commodity."
GREG GORDON, *Landscape of Desire*

In his introduction to *Desert Solitaire*, Edward Abbey warns
readers that his book is an elegy for the canyon country, not
a guide, a tombstone, not a birth certificate. Nine months
after I was born, Abbey died. Academics and activists have
written entire books eulogizing Ed, reminiscing about

encounters with the man and his words and debating the importance of his legacy. When a lover first took me to the small tourist town of Moab (population 5,000) and adjacent Arches National Park in Southern Utah, I hadn't read any of these books, Abbey's or anyone else's, and I wasn't aware that I was traveling to a landscape that had already been marked as dead by the man who claimed to love it most. Hiking the Delicate Arch with dozens of other tourists, I didn't know that I was walking through Ed's nightmare, that I should be irritated by the crowds and horrified by the "development" in the park. I never have known and never will know the desert wilderness of Arches that Abbey writes about in *Desert Solitaire*.

Regardless, I managed to fall in love with the diminished, overdeveloped, and over-visited landscape that is Arches. After that first trip I returned again and again to spend time in the Fiery Furnace and Devils Garden. I joined the multitudes countless times on the pilgrimage to Delicate Arch, eventually branching out of the park into other areas along the river and south of town. I wandered through Hidden Valley, Moonflower Canyon, Mary Jane Canyon, and Negro Bill Canyon. (This latter canyon used to have a more blatantly racist name until it was renamed in the 1960s. Its current appellation still makes me cringe, so I privately refer to it as Granstaff Canyon after William Granstaff, the African American cowboy who ran cattle there in the 1870s.) I roamed the areas surrounding Ken's Lake and Fisher Towers, kissed my lover under Bowtie Arch, traipsed up the Moab Rim and Porcupine Rim, and

stumbled drunk and joyful through sand and cacti to poke
at a fire and sing to the rocks in the dark way-back beyond
a friend's house. I swam in the Colorado along Potash Road
and waved to gaggles of grinning, middle-aged tourists on
jet boat tours, counted shooting stars while reclining on a
picnic table at Big Bend Campground, shook fire ants out
of my Keen sandals at Left Hand, and exchanged amused
glances with horses when I went running on sunny mornings in Spanish Valley. As time passed, I learned both to
feed off the energy of the summer crowds and to welcome
the quiet solitude of winter.

Love letter, Winter 2010: Disheartened by hours spent with
this blank page, I've given up on writing a poem for
you. Just like the desert, you've left me speechless and
grasping to find the words I normally use to describe
beauty. I suppose it's fitting. Even though you're not
here now, you did grow up visiting this small town
Abbey made famous, nursing a horizon of red rock,
white mountains, and blue sky, with the scent of juniper
in your hair and the grit of red dirt between your
teeth. Instead of writing, I've been warming my feet on
sandstone and waiting for the tourists to leave for the
winter. It is only then that the raven's call will regain
its resonance, and it is only then that I will spend short
days skirting canyon rims, looking for patches of sun
to sit in, and read your letters. I've been searching for
something out in the desert, and I don't know what it
is, but I hope I never find it so I can keep looking. Two

days ago I realized that the first time I ever saw clearly
was through an arch out in Devils Garden. Yesterday
I peered into a pothole in Hidden Valley, and a coyote
stared back. I'll admit that I haven't been writing, but
I've begun to grow a cactus in the bend of my left knee,
and I'm certain that the day you break my heart it will
bloom yellow . . .

On these subsequent trips I toted Abbey and other desert
writers along with me in my CamelBak. I savored books by
Terry Tempest Williams, Ellen Meloy, and Barry Lopez.
I read Jim Stiles's book on Moab, and T. H. Watkins's *The
Redrock Chronicles*. Reading these works, I learned the history
and politics of the region and found kindred spirits who
seemed to understand my feelings for the desert. I got to
know Ed secondhand from the edited collection of essays
by those who knew him: *Resist Much, Obey Little: Remembering
Ed Abbey*. I mourned for the man twenty years after his
death. Increasingly, I found myself musing on his warning
in the introduction to *Desert Solitaire*.

Despite his injunction against attempting to visit the
version of Arches he invokes in *Desert Solitaire*, I found that
I was one of many scraggly young people filing into Moab
clutching careworn copies of the book, vainly searching
for Abbey's country. Along with this observation came a
growing puzzlement and irritation. I couldn't ignore what I
interpreted as Abbey's insinuation that the desert "wilderness" I was growing to adore was a cheap and inauthentic
copy of the vibrant, living place he loved. I was haunted and

saddened by the knowledge of loss. I was also angry and frustrated that so many authors who write about Southern Utah adamantly and repeatedly inform younger readers like myself that the good old days were theirs and not ours. I longed to point out that Native Americans could conceivably make claims similar to Abbey's about the time before Euro-Americans showed up. More centrally, the rebellious and self-absorbed voice of my youth ached to demand that my elders validate and acknowledge my own experiences of the desert and Moab.

I understand the desire that Abbey and some of the other writers I listed above have to grieve for what has been lost in the process of developing Utah's national parks. I also understand that mass tourism has serious negative consequences for the environment and questionable implications for nearby towns. I do not disavow the possibility that we are loving the desert to death. Furthermore, I cannot deny that some days I wonder what it would be like to see Arches as Abbey saw it. However, I am also frustrated by trite dismissals of the current state of the American West and the way they devalue my own experience of nature. There is no ignoring the fact that I am a child of consumerist tourism. I was raised in the Pacific Northwest, and didn't see the desert until I was a young adult, living and studying in Salt Lake City. On my first visit to Southern Utah, I slept in a chain motel, ate breakfast at a trendy café, watched a short film on cryptobiotic soil at the visitor's center, and bought a bright orange Moab sweatshirt. My love for the desert was born on a group hike to Delicate Arch, not on a lone ramble, and while all of these things were largely out of my control, I also do not feel that my experience or affection are somehow diminished by these dubious beginnings. Regardless, like a self-conscious couple that met on an Internet matchmaking site, I find myself creating alternate, more "authentic" versions of my first date with the desert, versions that edit out the sweatshirt and the crowds and replace the chain motel with an open sky and the café with a pot of beans cooked over an open fire.

From my position within the conflicting arenas of environmentalism and consumer tourism, I am both embarrassed and defensive about the manner in which I came to know the desert. I am embarrassed because my experience does not fit within the typical nature-loving narrative of the solitary individual coming to appreciate the wild. I am also embarrassed that I so clearly participate in touristic consumerism. However, I am defensive because I was ignorant of the cultural dynamics and politics at play when I visited, and I don't know how I could have done things differently. I am also wary of norms that privilege certain nature experiences as more authentic or valuable than others. Abbey might shudder at present-day Arches, and Greg Gordon might dismiss Moab's current state as artificial and vapid, but they're mine and I love them possessively and defensively. I can't deny that there are times when the crowds test my patience and the profusion of eateries, hotels, and shops on Main Street seems obscene, but I also can't say that a crowd has ever ruined a hike for me, or that I've never been grateful for the culinary options available, charmed by a tacky souvenir, or not been entertained watching tourists and locals interact. Like any passionate love affair, my relationship with the area is complicated.

Love letter, Spring 2011: Tonight I stood on the edge of Porcupine Rim and watched the moon rise over Castle Valley. Gazing east reminded me of our hike to Fisher Towers, and the last time we were here together. We fought over how to divide our time between the town and the desert. You've never understood why I enjoy being on Main Street almost as much as in the canyons. It's just that I'm always certain if I spend enough time amid the gift shops and the hotels and the restaurants, I'll find that rasping but lovable vein of community that gives Moab its heart—and I usually do. Let's forget our fight, and just remember what came before. We drove in from Salt Lake City, and you rested your head on my shoulder and held my hand for the last twenty miles until we came around the bend and saw Moab light up the desert like all the promises we've made to each other and managed to keep . . .

I have a bumper sticker on the back of my car that says "I Love Moab." I also have two Moab sweatshirts, one coffee mug, a calendar, several posters, a trucker hat, three souvenir pens, a keychain, and a commemorative medal, shirt, and beer glass from October 2012's The Other Half—Moab Half Marathon. I'm ashamed and humiliated to admit that I own all of these things. I realize that they make me out to be the type of person many of my favorite desert writers would scorn and dismiss. I am contributing, quite consciously, to what people such as Gordon characterize as the commodification of nature. I purchase excessive amounts of outdoor gear and souvenirs in pursuit of a supposed communion with nature and sense of connection to Moab. The contradiction inherent in advertising my love for a rural town and the surrounding wilderness on the rear end of an oil-consuming machine that contributes to the degradation of the natural environment is not lost on me. When I ran The Other Half with more than one thousand other individuals, I was horrified by the sheer mass of us all, trotting in unison down Highway 128, decked out in our expensive neon running gear, leaving heaps of Dixie cups and wads of tissue in our wake. Some days I am so torn between my desire to preserve what is left of the desert and my guilty consumption and participation in mass tourism, I think that maybe the most responsible thing to do would be to just stay away.

However, once again, I also believe that my self-consciousness regarding the issue of defining responsible tourism and interactions with nature is the result of my understanding and complicity in an elitist vein of environmentalist thought that regulates and polices appropriate relationships with the natural world. I feel ashamed because I am not conforming to a proscribed set of behaviors and frugal consumption patterns that would reveal my love for the desert as true and authentic, clearly superior to the REI-outfitted masses, with their fanny packs and expensive cameras. The terrible truth is that while I feel a deep need to live a more sustainable lifestyle, I am not ready or willing to give up my Keen sandals or my CamelBak hydration system. I love my Moab souvenirs because it makes me happy to be reminded of the town during the long months I spend away. Furthermore, I don't feel as if my reliance on these items cheapens my passion for the desert or circumvents me from identifying with Abbey's writings. Every day brings a new navigation of my conflicting behaviors and beliefs. Some days when I encounter large numbers of other spandex-bedecked outdoor enthusiasts on the streets of Moab, I disavow any connection or affinity with *those* people, who clearly lack poetic love for the landscape and unscrupulously exploit it for the adrenaline rush and photo opportunities. Other days, I look at my reflection in the mirror, trendy and hip in Patagonia fleece and REI running tights, and feel a sense of disgust at my pretentious attitude. Who am I to pass judgment on anyone else's bond with the great Back of Beyond? As I said before, my relationship with Southern Utah and its inhabitants (both permanent and temporary) is complicated.

These days, I don't think of myself as a tourist, although it's a hard label to shake off. I lived in Moab on and off for six months, but that's hardly a moment in the eyes of many locals. Surrendering to the popular tendency to romanticize rural life, I'll confess that I've never felt as comfortable and at peace anywhere as I do in Moab. Writers such as Abbey, Gordon, Stiles, and Watkins in various ways acknowledge and reflect the popular tendency to gesture at Moab to illustrate the dangers of tourism and to offer a warning to other small western towns. Admittedly, the influx of second-home buyers has caused housing shortages, rapidly rising property values, and an overall increase in the cost of living that has severe negative consequences for many low-income individuals, and tourism adds a whole slew of other tensions and conflicts regarding resource allocation and the tenuous relationship between tourists and locals. However, I refuse to dismiss the town as a sellout or a has-been.

Yes, Moab has changed dramatically since Abbey's days, and not necessarily for the better, but Gordon's quick dismissal of the town is hardly fair and ignores the dynamic and multifaceted nature of the place. Once again, I stubbornly refuse to allow writers such as Abbey and Gordon to dictate and determine when a place has lost its authenticity and value. I adore Moab. I love the people, the smallness, and the pace of life. As soon as I roll into town I feel myself slow down and relax. The fact that I've lived there helps me dismiss the notion that I only feel this way because the town is my getaway, my vacation spot. During my last period of residency I worked at a local café and experienced my own share of high-season stress as I catered to seemingly never-ending lines of tourists demanding espresso and ice cream. Realistically, I know that a service-industry job is probably the most Moab could ever offer me. The reality is that the town's economy is fueled by tourism, and many people struggle to make ends meet in low-paying, seasonal jobs. Regardless, I dream of going back to stay.

Love letter, Summer 2011: I've barely left Moab and already
I miss you both like crazy. Maybe someday we'll stop
moving around the country and stay together in the
same place and time. I got your letter today, and smiled
when I saw "The Desert" bordered by two little hearts
in place of your name in the upper left-hand corner
of the envelope. I took the sprig of sagebrush you sent
and placed it in a glass bowl with the sand I gathered
in Hunter Canyon. On days when I'm feeling lost I
wrap my hands around that bowl and try to recall the
sensation of pressing my entire body against warm
sandstone. My tan lines are fading, but every time I
look at my arms I remember that time by the river when
you said my tattoos might as well be desert varnish,
and the memory pulls me closer to you and the land I
love . . .

I'm moving back to Moab in spring 2013. This will not
be a permanent relocation, but I simply can't stay away
anymore. I miss the town and the cliffs and the space. I tell
myself that if I can see red rocks every day and wander into
the desert whenever I desire, I'll be happy with a service-
industry job—for a while. I know that eventually I will
return to the city and begin the next phase of my career.
Perhaps I'll leave disillusioned and heartbroken, frustrated
by the tourists and pessimistic about the future of the desert. Maybe in a few years I'll be writing my own version of
Abbey's elegy, lamenting the continued development of the

area and warning off future generations. Maybe in a few decades I'll return to Moab from some far-off metropolis and curse and stomp my feet and declare that this isn't the desert that *I* loved. Then again, I don't think so. I want a definition of wilderness that is nebulous and expansive, an understanding and an ethic of nature that both values preservation for future generations, while also acknowledging the inevitability of change.

Despite my identification with Abbey and my affinity for his writing, I'm not searching for his wilderness. My identity and background dictate that my experience living in Moab will be vastly different from his, and I'm glad of that. I want to find my own vibrant, contemporary form of wilderness to love, and it isn't going to be anyone else's tombstone. As a queer, feminist Latina with a working-class background, I have a few bones to pick with ol' Ed, and if I bump into his ghost out on some mesa, I'll be quick to give him a piece of my mind. My understandings of ecofeminism, queer studies, environmental justice, disability studies, and postcolonialism demand that I look to wilderness and question the manner in which the concept relates to and supports misogynistic, homophobic, ableist, and racist forms of oppression. All too often, the American wilderness is associated with white, able-bodied, heterosexual, patriarchal masculinity to the exclusion of everyone else. Furthermore, my idea of wilderness questions the usefulness and ambiguity of a term that assigns value and worth to some landscapes while dismissing others as contami-

nated and unworthy of protection. What is both gained
and lost by valorizing wilderness? How do markers such as
class, race, gender, age, ability, and other factors dictate who
is privileged enough to appreciate and enjoy the supposed
benefits of a communion with nature? How can I form an
idea of wilderness that is inclusive of a wide array of people
with conflicting backgrounds and experiences and understandings of nature and the physical environment? How
can I balance my concern for these issues with my growing
sense of urgency and fear regarding the global environmental crisis? I don't know the answers to these questions, but
I'm tucking them in my CamelBak and carrying them with
me out into the desert, to scatter among the cacti and juniper, where I pray they'll be picked up and carried far and
wide by the lizards and ravens. Maybe they'll be found and
deciphered by some future generation, or perhaps they'll be
returned to me, delivered to my doorstep in the night by a
coyote and the wind. Until then, I haven't got time to wait
patiently, so if you need me I'll be out scouring the desert,
searching for answers.

Journal entry, Winter 2012: There is a scar on my lover's
right hip, from a playful encounter with a juniper tree
on the trail to Druid Arch. We spent five days roaming
Canyonlands National Park, predicting the behavior
of lizards and scrutinizing petroglyphs as if they held
the secret to keeping us together. I found a rattlesnake
flattened perpendicular to the highway's yellow line,
and we took it as a bad omen. Our thoughts collected

like raindrops in a sandstone depression. The word they finally formed was "goodbye," so we divvied up our love and parted ways. That was over a year ago, and the cactus in the bend of my knee has bloomed and withered, but I'm too busy planting seeds to write any elegies.

Sunset at Mile 16

Alycia Parnell

Here is a story to break your heart.

Sometimes words get stuck in my head like songs. It's often just one syllable, other times a half-sentence or a quarter-thought. In this case, the line from a Mary Oliver poem comes out of nowhere, like spinning red-and-blue lights in your rearview mirror when, for a minute, you forget who you are and press the gas pedal just because it's there. I'm not the most ardent reader of Mary Oliver—too much stuff about birds—but this poem's opening line repeats itself in my mind with every returning glance up to the desert sunset. Sherbet hues drift from the blackening razor skyline of mountains— here is a story—the watchtower profile of Baboquivari Peak crisped by impending night—to break your heart.

The U.S. Fish and Wildlife Service sent me to work at Buenos Aires National Wildlife Refuge, an hour and a half south of Tucson, the closest place to get decent coffee and vegetables or to see someone you could imagine letting into your living room. They have me mapping plants whose Latin names I'm supposed to know—the project is something about saving the masked bobwhite quail. As with a vast portion of our nation's semiarid grasslands, this region of southern Arizona's Altar Valley was overgrazed in the late 1800s. Drought hit, and the bovine interlopers chewed up the tender green blades of anything vaguely grassy, crushing root systems with each clumsy step, until the grass defied everyone's expectations by actually running out and brushy clutter like mesquite took over the land.

For a century, ecological relationships based on the grasses suffered, until authorities pinpointed one adorable poster child for the cause of restoring the valley: the masked bobwhite quail. These softball-sized, glassy-eyed puffs of earth-colored down were nearly extinct after the grasses that they depended on for food and shelter were destroyed. These pudgy, ground-dwelling birds were seen as worthy of resurrection, and a national wildlife refuge was born. Since then, grass has made a comeback, though much of it is invasive. The bobwhite quail seem to be slowly accepting the fact that they don't have to become extinct, though they still require highly regulated breeding environments and release into sites that are nothing less than ideal. It's progress, but it isn't perfect, especially with limited resources.

Buenos Aires and other refuges often rely on volunteer power to function, which is how recent graduates like me with no other viable employment offers end up on the

Mexico border. According to the U.S. Fish and Wildlife Service, I'm providing inventory and monitoring services to quantify critical quail habitat. Really, I just follow a red circle on a lemon-colored GPS unit through pock-marked grasslands and rocky washes and every kind of vegetation that hurts, including but not limited to Sonoran ocotillo forests, the ill-named teddy bear cholla, and the still-ubiquitous mesquite. My circle almost always leads me under low-hanging *Senegalia greggii*, the tree formerly known as *Acacia greggii*, before botanists pruned the genus. The new name, like many others, isn't in the field guide they gave me. I quickly learned that normal people just call it "cat's claw" for a reason.

I can hear a breeze before I feel it, whispering through the drying seed heads of grasses and mesquite pods in the distance before coming my way to provide fleeting relief from the desert temperatures. The surrounding plants respond to my every step, producing sharp rattles in the depths of thorned bushes that always conjure a split moment of panic while I distinguish the dry hiss of grasshoppers from more lethal warnings from one of the five resident rattlesnake species. It's a great job, really. I work outside, doing something related to my idealistic degree. I have a tan. Sweating in my uniform is encouraged, if not mandatory.

I'd like to say that I go places to which no person has traveled before, but that's not true. The refuge lies on the U.S.-Mexico border between Nogales to the east and Organ Pipe Cactus National Monument to the west. Like the majority of borderlands located within a few days' walk in the desert sun to a U.S. highway, it is a main corridor of transit for people coming north from Mexico. In our law enforcement training, we were told that the travelers do not want to be seen, but are usually armed just in case they need to be, especially in the mountains, where the drug runners go. The training officer stood before us in the air-conditioned training room and gravely informed us that they sometimes have machine guns. I can't imagine the financial feasibility of procuring a machine gun for the majority of people willing to walk for three days in 103-degree heat to pick fruit for minimum wage, but what do I know. I've never looked at prices. The only machine guns I'd ever seen were strapped to the Border Patrol agents themselves. At any rate, we were told to stay away from any signs of human activity in the field, and to alert Border Patrol immediately if we see any humans who shouldn't be there. They call them UDAs, since saying "undocumented alien" is inefficient. Another favorite is the illegitimate noun version of "illegal." Sometimes they're aptly dubbed "walkers." The ones who walk until they can't anymore are "quitters." They're never called people.

I haven't come in contact with anyone yet, but I was told that would likely change once autumn sets in and temperatures sink from the hellish peaks of summer. This doesn't mean that they're not walking now, though. The signs are everywhere when we go into the field with our water bladders, sunscreen, and GPS units. As if the problems with the refuge's ecology associated with grazing and invasive species weren't enough, the land also serves the purpose of a public garbage can for people walking north. It's a diluted landfill. You can't take ten steps without seeing something nonnative—a camouflage-patterned bandanna trampled into the near-sterile earth beside a patch of *Salsola tragus*, fields of *Eragrostis lehmanniana* and *Sorghum halepense* strewn with torn clothing, an occasional sandal or bicycle tire, blister packs of caffeine pills or other stimulants, and countless chipped water bottles . . . always empty. Under the same shade trees where walkers have waited out the scorching daylight hours, I try to unscramble the spellings of Latin words. We're discouraged from using common names. The people are illegal and the plants are invasive. None of them are supposed to be on the refuge, but they've sought it anyway.

Sometimes the cover of the refuge isn't enough to see the walkers through their journeys. The law enforcement guys talked about the people who turn up on the side of the road, waiting for a Border Patrol truck to come along and pick them up. They don't care about going north anymore. All they want is *agua* and shade. One agent told the story of a quitter who stumbled to the asphalt of Highway 286, baked and beaten by the desert, and passed right by the bemused officer before crawling beneath the running engine of the big white Border Patrol truck with the green stripe and the cage in the back. It was the closest thing to shade he'd come across since dawn burned away the respite of the previous night.

Just past Mile 16 on Highway 286 sits a large bus. It's one of those behemoths with flights of stairs and excessive storage space often seen slowing highway traffic under the weight of adventurous senior citizens or traveling high school orchestras. This bus isn't quite for sightseeing, though. It sits there all day with the engine on to power the air-conditioning that makes the driver's shift bearable. The sole purpose of the silver-and-white bus with heavily tinted windows is to collect the quitters, walkers, and traffickers who encounter the green-suited Border Patrol throughout any given day. When I pass the bus, the driver is usually sitting inside at the wheel, performing some unknown task for however many hours before it's time to ship the poor sods home. Sometimes, I spot him standing on the sepia patch of bare earth that's been scraped clean of vegetation to accommodate the vehicle. I've seen him stretching his unused muscles, hunching over an awkward triangle of stiff legs. Stretching, as if he's taffy, or a walker, someone who really needs to stretch. Not that stiff muscles would be at the top of a walker's list of problems. I wonder what a person looks like after going long enough without water to give up on the dream of north. His skin, his tongue. Eyes still the color of earth spiked with rain—what do they look like at Mile 16?

Buenos Aires is a land of quitters and quail, though they are at odds with one another. It's hard to care about a largely flightless bird with a brain the size of half a shelled peanut when someone walking north has died for no reason within five miles of where you're standing. Of course, it's hard to care about people dying when people are dying everywhere. They do it in other countries. They do it in books. Sometimes they do it because they choose to, and these people chose to walk. It's hard to care when you have work to do.

Mary Oliver stops haunting me when I look back at the road after taking note of the sunset's progress and the presence of the idling bus shining in the waning light. I have a book of hers, despite the birds. I briefly look forward to flipping through it to find the current poem of interest before my memory confronts me with sinking dismay. I hadn't brought it to Arizona with me. I'd left it in my home library in Utah, not thinking I'd want it.

I console myself with the poetry of other, more land-based creatures. While roaming my new Sonoran home, I was engulfed with pure glee the first time I saw a pudgy, Halloween-colored Gila monster scuttling across my path. Whenever I see darkling beetles, I cup them in my hands and let them explore the terrain of my arms before depositing them out of the way of mountain bikers. I consider venomous snakes great neighbors. I tend to fall for things that disgust others. So when I snap out of my sunset reverie and see a small black knot of legs creeping into the road, my heart rattles with simultaneous joy and horror as I realize that it is the first tarantula I've ever seen in the flesh, and that I haven't spotted it in time to avoid crushing it beneath my car's front right tire. I'm going 72 in a 55-mph zone, and not because I'm not paying attention. The moment passes in an instant, and I glance with mute shock at the half-paved tarantula in my rearview mirror, its front set of legs bound to asphalt. I'm sobered by my indiscretion and send the equivalent of a prayer to Mary Oliver, who would surely have something to say about the matter. I offer myself the double-edged consolation that worse atrocities have occurred in this desert.

I slow down at mile marker 7 and take a sharp left at the big brown sign indicating that the refuge headquarters can be found three miles down the road. Two dirt miles past that is the government trailer where I am housed for the duration of my contract. I pull up to the trailer just past the sunset's color show and unload my supplies for the week— beer, discount cheese, salted foods for the field. I lock the car and walk toward the front steps with my cargo but stop short when I see a small dark splotch on the pale weathered siding of the trailer. Hairy, lots of legs. Another tarantula, gloriously living, sprawled upon my home and delicately tapping its surface in search of some dark corner or another. Briefly, I'd been redeemed—the creature that bore my sin had been reborn.

So here is a story to break your heart. At some point that evening, the bus driver stepped back into his wheeled silver cage and drove its cargo from Mile 16 to the end of the world. The first tarantula is still dead, now long digested by some desert scavenger. My book of Mary Oliver poems is somewhere familiar, and I am in a place where people die. And the sun doesn't care, and will make the sky beautiful again in the morning, as if nothing had happened.

Birdhouse Treasures

William Thomas

I stood on the crumbling retaining wall looking at an abandoned urban block in Baltimore. The ground was covered with trash, and there were three houses on the corner with caved-in roofs and collapsing brick walls. Their doors were long gone, and the windows were just rotting sills with warped frames and shards of glass stuck in the glazing. "It's perfect," I mumbled to myself. I saw what others had overlooked. These houses could be fixed, and I could shelter friends, build kitchens, rebuild bathrooms, put in woodstoves, and create meeting spaces for the Collective. Everyone would rally together and we would be unstoppable.

We shaped our community garden with thousands of hours of work: volunteers pushing shovels through the dirt, pushing stones into place, sifting and tilling soil, and planting seeds. As a group with nothing to lose, we collected all the tools we could gather, pushing ourselves to build what would become Baltimore Free Farm. I fed this machine the materials we needed to sustain the energy.

A few blocks away, I found the source for the materials needed to build the farm and restore the houses: a huge abandoned building. The front door was barricaded and the windows had boards over them, so I went around the back to see if I could find another way in. The building loomed over me as it has over everyone else who has walked past it on this busy street for many years. Something told me the good stuff was inside. Curiously protruding in search of sunlight, a tree grew between the joints of the brickwork two stories off the ground between blown-out windows. "Aha!" I thought to myself as I leaned a discarded sofa against the building to get at a small window on the first level. The upper glass pane was broken, so I was able to reach my arm in and unlock the window. I minded the shards, and any onlookers, then pulled myself inside.

The first couple of steps in a building like this are always cautious and deliberate. Even after going through this sequence as many times as I have it never changes: you squat down low, close your eyes, and listen. The echoes of cooing pigeons mean this is a wild place, and the sound of automobile traffic outside and life going on as usual for the rest of the world means I am unnoticed. Taking a controlled breath, I inhale the stillness in the air. I am alone. Meandering through the building around the scattered remains of lives lived makes me wonder about when this place was full of people. The colors in my vision grow grainy like in old movies, and I stand as an invisible voyeur, watching the workers a hundred years ago busy in the space. I follow them about their routines like an employee on the first day following a trainer until the visions vanish into thin air, and I am back, and the colors are back to normal. My explorative nature has introduced me to all sorts of destinations that are not on the tourist map of Baltimore. Shuttered factories, warehouses, and homes that have been sitting for decades unused; these places are a scavenger's orchard ripe for the picking. I have long thought that the new frontier is not out in the Wild West or someplace far north; it's right here in the empty spaces around us, waiting to be tamed.

I marvel at the building I am in. Twenty-foot-high ceilings and large arched brick doorways transition from room to room. The lead paint peeling off the walls and its dust blowing out the empty window frames into the neighborhood are homage to the century-gone painters who applied the paint, the dust like their ashes scattered from a mountaintop. Old hardwood floors creak as I walk about them, breaking the silence and confirming my presence to myself. As I click on my flashlight and explore the basement level, a cold cement floor deadens the sound of my footsteps and the total silence makes me afraid of disappearing into the darkness. Here, a long-decommissioned oil-fired boiler furnace looms over me large enough to fit a small school bus inside. The amount of human energy it took to build this place is humbling. This was an abandoned badge-making factory right around the corner from where I live. Built in the 1800s, the place for decades made badges for police and firemen up and down the East Coast. Now it's home to wild birds.

Some of those birds, startled as I walk to the upper level, jump to flight in frenzy. Seeing a human in this space is something that must be rare for them because they react in a panic, flying everywhere, trying to escape through open windows, crashing into closed ones. When things calm down I find a pigeon that has crashed and broken its neck, still warm. The next time I come here I will try harder not to startle them.

I start my work by approximately counting things and stating them out loud to myself. I make a list in my head of all the reusable building materials throughout the badge factory. A structure like this is made up of hundreds of different parts. Electrical conduits, plumbing fittings, loose bricks, wood trim, doorknobs, and hinges are just some of the things that most people see as fixtures and hardly even notice. Decades of wild men and animals have ransacked this place and the good parts were left untouched. I knew what this place was now. It was my treasure chest. The living community that I am a part of awaits material goods like pigeon chicks in the nest crying out for nuts and bolts. We need all these pieces of "property," to build our lives and our community in a vision like ourselves—free. The people in the community I am a part of are free and will never own each other or these material things we use daily without noticing. So what is theft of property to those who see property as theft itself?

As usual, in my first encounter I will leave empty-handed from a space like this. All the things here couldn't be used right away or even stored in my community's nest. The world is our warehouse. None of these things is going anywhere. I come back for things as they are needed, heisting them away to become part of something living, leaving the dormancy that time sold them into. They are little bits of string and stick to build the nest carried one beak-full at a time.

I retrace my steps out the window and climb down the sofa. I pitch the sofa on its side and walk down the block back to my home, feeling much richer. This birdhouse treasure chest is one of many scattered throughout the city. These different buildings have served to keep the dream of freedom afloat.

As deeply as I try to scratch the surface of things to eke it all out for community, I realize the depth of the surface is far greater than I ever imagined. I used to think I could crash through it and get to the bottom of things. I thought the world was a replenishing resource of everything humanity could ever need. This is not true. These buildings we have all built and abandoned, into which trees sink their roots and birds set their claws, are symptomatic of a disorder. Ownership of anything is temporary; the wild will come to take it back.

Erosion/Accretion

Amelia Urry

At dawn, I can hear the waves. They crash against the beach about a quarter mile out, but from here the sound is as measured and calm as the breath of the body lumped in the narrow twin bed next to my mine. Lily is asleep. The other bodies in the crude wooden cabins arranged across the lawn are asleep, suspended in the interminable moment before the sun breaks over the horizon and plates the sea with silver. Then we will see the long lines of whitewater unfolding matter-of-factly toward the beach, grinding boulders into pebbles in one sustained note of impact, drawing back with a hiss of release, breathing endlessly in and out.

We are perched on the green point of Cape Breton Island, in Nova Scotia, a few miles outside the closest town (population 48), at the end of a rutted dirt road, right at the edge of the water. To the north is a large saltwater lagoon that

feels the tides but not the surf. The Atlantic lies to the east
and south, buffered by a strip of rocky beach that, except
for two gaps where the sea pours back and forth, protects
us from the waves.

Grandpa built this place when our parents were still
surly teenagers, and kept building it the rest of his life. He
designed the strange, octagonal cabins with their pleated
roofs and enormous, sealed ship windows, shingled them,
painted them with whitewash and tar. He built the main
cabin with its precarious water tower overlooking the point,
the boathouse jutting on spindly struts over our little lake-
side beach, the skeleton of Cove House-to-be rising from
the long grass at the edge of the lawn. Our scruffy little
piece of the earth. He named it Limesean, the way old families used to name their grand estates and summer homes:
Tara, Talland House.

The tiny handprints of grandchildren are pressed into
the concrete foundations; traditions, also, set early. These
sheets on that bed, this pillow. Norman comes by in the
morning to drink his cup of coffee and talk over the headlines. When Grandpa makes jam, the kids stir.

We walk out to the bench in the evening with Grandma,
who smokes her cigarette and watches the sea. The sun sets
behind us, over a black line of pine trees and the bright
reflection of the lake, but we stare out at the dark waves
rippling out under the purpling sky. "One day this will be
oceanfront property," she tells us, gesturing to the fringe
of field sloping down to the water. "In a hundred years, it'll
come all the way to our doorstep."

The landscapes I love were all made in collapse. The big red scarp by the beach on the long walk out to the Head was once a hill sloping smoothly down to the water. The Head itself, a grassy knob of stone left jutting up from the sea, is tethered to land only by a thin causeway that appears and disappears with the tide. Whole stands of pine trees cant down like broken bristles, their exposed roots like bleached bone, clutching at a retreating shoreline. The devastation of these things was perfect once; then it kept changing.

Year after year, the Gut is getting bigger. That vulnerable gap in the barrier beach slowly settles into a low, toothless grin where the waves come in now even at low tide, foam fizzing out among the pebbles where once the high-humped back of the beach shuddered under the invisible pounding of the surf. On our side of the beach, the lake is filling in with sand. At low tide, we can walk from the back door of the boathouse across the broad sandbar, to where the channel carves out the last thin line of resistance between us and the island. Our feet don't even get wet.

I learn the words later, after I already know what is happening. The summers get warmer, the berries come earlier. The piercing cold of the mornings becomes a story we tell each other on the sunny, white-hot afternoons, when we really wish someone had thought to make windows that could open. I'm still young enough that ten or fifteen years of observing this place isn't a scientific sample size, but it does happen to overlap with ten or fifteen years of extraordinary change. Heat waves sweep across continents, droughts last longer and longer, the concentration of carbon dioxide in the atmosphere inches higher than it's ever been before.

When Grandpa is dying, we only have time to say "I love you" once, the last time we take him home from the hospital. The unhealable sore on his leg, the crooked joint of the finger reattached in childhood, the stump of a toe lost later, all these outward marks glossed over a deeper degeneration as one by one his organs stopped. Afterward, Grandma sold their house but kept Limesean. The last time we were all up there together, we scattered his ashes over the berry field with a soupspoon.

One summer, between guests, I am alone up there for two days. It is the first time this place has ever felt lonely. So much changes, but the insides stay largely the same: the white, porous bones scavenged from the high-water line at the end of the harsh winters, arrayed along the walls of the main cabin—shoulder blades, jawbones, ribs, the wide-socketed skulls of birds. The whale vertebra rests by the back door, as large as a car tire. Old buoys and kites hang on the wall above the bookshelves, and in the corner an old baby doll, rescued from the high-tide line, spins lazily by her heel, wide-eyed and familiar as an old chandelier.

I take the kayak out onto the lake one afternoon. When I get far enough away from the house, it is just an empty box whose big windows flash, then disappear. I cannot tell which one of us has come unmoored. That night, I feel like the last person in the world.

Our mailbox is long gone; now the turnoff for our driveway is marked by a large yellow sign advertising a German development company that last year plowed out a whole tract of forest, built two houses on the opposite side of the spit, then seemed to vanish. I give it the *malocchio* my grandmother trained us to do when these signs first started appearing around here years ago.

When my boyfriend comes, we sleep in the boathouse, on the big bed my grandfather built. The first night, I leave the blinds open so that the sun will spill in when it comes up bright and unmediated over the Atlantic. In the light, I feel suddenly shy as I show him the small cabins, their splintered edges, the treasures laid along their shelves. We have spent the summer apart, but here it feels like more than that, like I have spent my entire life pacing this little corner of sea and land. "Is this where you used to sleep?" he asks me, leading me over to the little bed. "Did you used to look out this window?" I watch the deep blue patch of sky in the window and hold him tightly as the story is rewritten in my head.

We stay naked when we can. It is an unusually hot summer, and anyhow there is no one around to see us as we wave and dance behind the big windows. We read during the day, feet up in my grandmother's chair or curled on the daybeds, peeling clementines. He is my first boyfriend, and this is the first time we've spent away from friends, away from family. I find myself following him and straightening the objects that he places askew, fitting each item into the slot memory has left for it. One day, Norman takes us jigging for mackerel in his lobster boat, then shows us how to filet the small, jewel-like fish with a kitchen knife. Michael and I make dinner in the crooked kitchen, and cook too much for the two of us to eat. The wine is sharp as vinegar, but we drink it anyway and watch night creep in from the sea.

When I turn out the lights and lie in the familiar dark, I can feel the whole of Limesean still sprawled around me. It holds all of the old ghosts: Grandpa making pancakes with the wild blueberries we picked, checking his blood sugar in the morning. Pearl down the road with her maple cookies. Jimmy's bucket of spit behind the couch. Eileen and Joanne stirring jellyfish soup under the jetty that washed away one winter. The now-toppled water tower making its crooked silhouette against the sky at sunset. The notch in the shoreline where a large whirlpool used to form, a wheel of foam spinning at the center.

We fall asleep listening to the waves.

III.
MINDFUL
MONKEYWRENCHING

Diseases of Affluence

Ben Cromwell

"There's a sale on cribs," she says, "at Babies 'R' Us. It's only $200 for a crib that converts into a full-size bed." I grunt in return. "That's a really good deal."

It probably is, but I'm having trouble getting into baby shopping. We are still six months from having a baby, and I am alarmed by the sheer volume of stuff that is beginning to accumulate in preparation for our son. To be fair, we've not bought most of it yet. A great deal of it exists only in my mother's and mother-in-law's minds.

"Make us a list," my mother says. "People will be asking what you want soon." The idea that other people will end up buying most of these things for us, and an even better notion that we'll get quite a lot of it secondhand from my sister-in-law who has had three babies and called it quits, is somewhat reassuring, but the whole concept is slightly overwhelming all the same.

One needs so much shit to have a baby these days: crib, changing table, rocking chair, high chair, swing, sling, car seat, stroller, baby carrier, diaper pail, diapers, baby bath, breast pump, bottles, bibs, nooks, outfits, pajamas, hats, bonnets, diaper bag, not to mention all the toys and books, plus blankies that every member of my immediate and extended family will shortly be knitting.

"How are we supposed to know what we'll want or need?" asks Raven. "We've never had a baby before." I nod.

Raven has decided to go back to school a few months after having our baby. Among the schools she's looking at are the University of Oregon, Arizona State, and the University of New Orleans. "You're going to move right after you have a baby?" people ask, as though something like this has never been done. "I don't think you understand how much harder it is to do things like that with a baby around. You should really stay close to your parents."

Raven and I have lived without electricity or running water when we were Peace Corps volunteers in Kiribati, hiked more than 2,000 miles on the Appalachian Trail, and worked as educators with every age group of children there is, and yet people insist that we are unprepared for parenthood. On one level, this scares me profoundly. On another, I question the child-rearing techniques and practices of those who claim that taking care of a child is paramount to any other conceivable hardship.

"I loved you when you were born, but I wasn't really into you. Not like I was with your sister. As soon as she came out, I was in love with her. She was so beautiful." My father smiles at this point in the retelling, a watery and sentimental smile. I am momentarily jealous.

"I didn't really get into you so much until you were about three years old. That winter I took you sledding. We climbed up that hill down by the bike path—the one near the soccer fields. You had this blue plastic sled, and we got to the top and you sat down in it and I pushed you." He pauses, remembering the moment, and I remember, too. I can't remember the incident at all, but I remember the hill. We used to do wind sprints up it in cross-country because it was the steepest hill around, and it was long, probably a hundred yards, with a long, flat plain below.

"You went about fifty feet, and then the sled turned sideways and flipped and you went flying, and I thought, 'Oh shit, he might be dead.' But then you sat up in the snow and waved. I was so relieved."

"That's when you first loved your child?" My wife is incredulous. We are sitting in my parents' dining room. My mom is preparing dinner in the kitchen. The three of us are seated around the table discussing the prospect of grandchildren.

"That was the first time I really got it, that he was a real person."

"Before that you thought he was just some kind of toy?" He shrugs and smiles in a way that says "It is what it is." Raven looks like she wants to say something else. She's obviously upset by this information.

"You'd better love your grandchildren instantly," says Raven, "otherwise you won't be allowed to see them."

"I'll love them," Dad says in a sappy sort of voice that is nevertheless sincere. I roll my eyes.

My father didn't want to be a father in 1981. He wanted to travel the world. He had been a Peace Corps volunteer in Nepal in the 1970s, a teacher like Raven and I would become, and returned to find, as we did three decades later, that America was not the place he'd thought it was. In his village, he'd lived off of seasonal vegetables, dried lentils, and rice. Meat was served very occasionally for festivals, and almost every bit of traveling he'd done had been on foot. Back at home, the sheer number of people in the stores and on the streets confused and disoriented him. Politics seemed hopelessly corrupt, and the world itself seemed callous and cold. The solution, he thought, was to go back overseas. Instead, he got a job with the federal government, married my mother, and had me.

"I took a trip last summer down Route 66," he says. "Me and Frank climbed into the Plymouth and drove from Chicago to California. When we got there, we split up. Frank wanted to get back to Chicago after three days, but I stayed for a month."

He looks down and begins to pet the black Lab at his side absentmindedly. "Shadow was there, too." He laughs at this, and I do, too. "That was a long time ago," he says, "back before I met your grandmother."

He smiles. "I think I'll go to bed."

My grandfather pushes slowly up from the wooden chair

he's in and wobbles a little. He begins walking toward his bedroom, pauses, turns aside toward the cabinets. He opens one and takes out a short glass. "You want a Scotch?" he says.

"We just had one," I say. "See, your glass is over at the end of the table."

"Oh yeah," he says, and he laughs. "Well, I guess I'll have one more. You want one?"

"All right," I say. He goes to the liquor cabinet and takes down the bottle and fills his glass, then he passes me the bottle and returns to the other end of the table. He sits down and takes a long pull of his drink.

"That's good," he says. We sit in silence for a moment, and I look around at the kitchen. It's so familiar to me. My grandparents have lived here for more than ten years, and before that, every object in this kitchen had been positioned in almost the exact same arrangement as in their old house. This house is located in rural Illinois, north of Rockford. Their old house was in a suburb of Chicago. The dog, gray in the muzzle and rather fat, is a relatively recent acquisition. She used to live with my parents in southern Illinois. They brought her up here when they moved to Salt Lake City. Grandpa scratches her ears.

"Did I ever tell you about the time me and Shadow drove out to California?"

I smile.

Alzheimer's is a disease of affluence. My grandparents are not rich. They struggle to get by. The term is relative. It describes diseases that people are more prone to the longer they live. My grandfather has had it for almost a decade. Little by little, I see him going. He is no longer the sharp, funny man he used to be. He's lost the nuanced parts of his personality. He sleeps most of the time, waking for a few hours to eat and sit in his chair in the kitchen, and he has become dependent on my grandmother for everything.

"Grammy?" he calls plaintively, when he wants something, and she, for her part, caters to his wishes. She cannot stand to see this man she loves so reduced. Both of them are scared and they cling to each other, to their old habits and routines, but as the disease progresses, even those get lost. The other day, my grandmother told me that he had completely forgotten who she was for the first time. She sat with him and explained that she was his wife, tried to jog his memory with photographs and the names of their children. They both ended up crying.

I love my father, have always loved him, but I wasn't really "into him" for a while. Perhaps that's why I'm okay with the fact that he wasn't into me either. Love is a fierce emotion. It comes of instinct between parent and child, but there is a deeper kind of love more closely related to respect, which must be learned.

We used to work out together. On Sundays we would ride our bikes down to the track at the Southern Illinois Edwardsville campus and then run a mile before biking back. I admit to being completely lame at this. My bike was slightly too big for me, a brand-new eighteen-speed hybrid, and I didn't understand how to work the shifters, so I rode constantly in one gear, simply pedaling harder on the hills. When we got to the track, I would often whine or whimper as we ran. The mile was difficult for me. There was also this trick to mounting a bike that my dad tried to teach me. You put one foot on the pedal and push off to get going, and then swing your leg over the seat and get your other foot situated. I could not get the hang of it.

My father got upset each time we engaged in the ritual of Biathlon Sunday. We'd start off well, but by the fourth stoplight, my awkward starts and stops would begin to get on his nerves and he would demonstrate the procedure to me over and over in the hope that I would pick it up. At the track, my whining tried his patience. On the way home, he would ridicule me about using the gears. In another part of my mind, I return to these memories, trying to reconstruct my childhood, so I can figure out how to cobble something together for my own child. Is this what parenting is? Is it creating some struggle, even though we don't have to fish for our living? Is it finding conflict in the suburbs, where the slightest traces of it have been removed?

Alzheimer's is terminal, irreversible. My grandfather will die of it.

I've thought that I should not have a child at all. What if I develop Alzheimer's disease and he has to care for me? What if he develops it himself? What if my worst fears come true and we are all left starving and impoverished from climate change? And there are other more conventional terrors to be reckoned. What if he becomes a serial killer? What if he doesn't love us? What if he develops a coke habit or never learns to make meaningful relationships? What if he ends up in poverty? "Stay in there," I think. "Just stay where you are and let us keep pretending."

I've thought these things and convinced myself that this is surely a mistake. But he will come. Raven and I will be parents, and he will come and become. I have to hold myself back, have to breathe. It is all right not to know the future. It is all right to step into the unknown, and my fear is inconsiderate. He will be enough.

When we lived in Kiribati, our island was called Abaiang. It is going underwater. In just a few decades, nothing of the island will be left but a few rocks visible at low tide. Kiribati is one of the first countries that will be erased from the face of the earth by climate change.

My friend Tebwake died on Abaiang. This is how it happened. He walked out of his bathroom one morning and fell over. I saw the other men in the village running toward his house and I ran with them. I felt for a pulse. It was faint, but still present. We scooped him up into the back of a truck that had stopped near the village. I rode with him to the medical station keeping my fingers on his wrist. He was pale, chalky, his hands and feet clammy.

We massaged his extremities trying to get the blood to circulate, but his pulse got weaker and weaker and when we finally arrived at the clinic and the nurse's aide listened to his chest with her stethoscope, there was nothing to hear.

Tebwake was dead. In my journal, there is a poem and a letter I wrote to my parents about the incident, how strange and spooky it was to feel a man die beat by beat and know there was nothing to be done about it.

I stayed with him when they brought him back to his home and watched as his wife washed the body. She found a gray pair of briefs and slid them up over his thighs, tucked his balls into the waistband and worked the elastic over his hips and buttocks. She did this smiling, and even laughed a little while handling his genitals. It was too much for me.

I don't know the exact cause of death for Tebwake, but I'm almost certain it was massive heart failure. There was no qualified doctor on the island to perform an autopsy, and it wouldn't have mattered anyway. He died of rich food, beer, kava. He died because there was no doctor to give him a checkup. He was in his thirties.

Heart disease is also considered to be a disease of affluence though no one would argue that Tebwake was rich. It is related to poor nutritional choices. Poor people aren't supposed to have access to the type of diet that leads to heart attacks. Only relatively affluent societies can afford poor nutrition.

At his wake, people took pictures of the body. Some even posed with it as though he were still alive. Raven and I could hardly keep from crying. We'd never seen something like this, so little mediation between the living and the dead.

Two classmates of mine died in a car accident when I was in high school. They were driving a brand-new red Jeep

Cherokee on a country road, and it flipped as they took a turn at speed. Neither of them was wearing a seat belt. I went to Marcus's wake. His body was in a casket in front of the altar of the Catholic church he attended. The attendees filed slowly past, and I had a bizarre impulse to reach out and touch his heavily made-up face. He was so strange. In some ways no changes had taken place at all. He was preserved in a chemical soup, would remain sixteen forever. In other ways, he was unrecognizable. I had not known him well, but I'd seen him around, and his face was paler, puffier than it had been in life. He was stiff; he'd lost all the elasticity in his skin and joints, the strange spark that had made him human.

Tebwake began to putrefy on the second day, began turning from solid to liquid. We put him in the ground with a sense of relief.

We lived close to something primal on Abaiang. Perhaps it was the fact that there was so little land and so much sea, the improbability of life itself establishing a foothold here, on such a tiny speck of land. You could not help but be awed when you stared off into the vast blue void at the tip of the island. There was a largeness to it, an immensity of scale that I cannot adequately capture.

To be that close to the edge of the world inspires a kind of connection to it. There is so little here. Literally, we were on an island of life in the middle of the sea, and we're on it still, though it is less obvious how close to the edge of the world we are. Maybe that's the real disease of affluence: deception, the gilt frame that hides how close we all are to inundation. Everyone dies. My trust in the Earth stems from this. We know, irrevocably, how this is going to end, and each time it doesn't is a kind of reprieve, a stay of execution. Collectively, this defiance is what bonds us, what brings us together. It is the basis of trust, which is really only denial. These lies that we will be all right.

We're going with a secondhand crib. We went over and checked it out last night. Friends of ours, Larry and Jess, have a five-year-old and a three-year-old, and they're ready, at last, to give up their old things. In addition to the crib we can have our pick of diaper bags, baby carriers, a high chair, and various clothes and toys.

"All this stuff is sort of overwhelming," I say. We're in Larry's kitchen. Their two kids, Marc and Eric, are in the living room watching *Dino Train*. Jess is still at work.

"It is," he says. "But you'll figure out what you need. Everyone's experience is different. When we were first pregnant with Marc, people asked us what we wanted, what we were registered for, and we were like, 'We've already got a BabyBjörn. That's pretty much all we think we'll need.' Obviously, we were wrong, but you figure it out."

We thank him and head for the door.

"Congratulations," he says, and he smiles at us with a kind of sympathy or understanding. I try my best to return the look.

"Thanks."

Once in the car, I turn to Raven. "He seemed so cheerful tonight. What's up with that?" Larry and Jess are usually aloof when we talk to them. They are of a different social caste. Jess is a doctor and Larry is an engineer, so they are rich compared to us, and they're usually too involved with their children to pay us much heed. Tonight's comments and advice are downright effusive by comparison.

"We're in the club now," says Raven. "We've been tricked into having kids, too, so now there's something to talk about. Plus they're experts and they're passing on their knowledge. It always makes people keen to talk when they can dispense advice."

I am disturbed by her comments. I don't want to be "in the club." The club seems wasteful, destructive, and deluded. Just think of all the crap that comes with being in the club, all the disposable diapers and clothes that get worn for a month and then thrown away. I have a brief flash of my grandfather and how all this will end.

"Larry was right about one thing," I say. "We'll figure it out."

"Of course we will. Team Ben and Raven and the baby," she says, and we drive off into the night.

The Lives of Plovers

Sierra Dickey

I live in a place of geological truisms. Here on the outer reaches of Cape Cod, where change is the only constant, you can never step onto the same beach twice. Every winter, the Gulf Stream goes about sluicing up sediment here and sucking away sand there. The Cape is continually nipped and tucked into new iterations. But such is the fate of glacial leftovers, landforms that lack the heavy anchor of a continent.

Curious creatures inhabit a place of such dynamism. One of them is the piping plover—the angel of our place. A small white dancer, she is also a messenger. But unlike the cherubs of God, who are vessels, the plover embodies truth in motion. Her form and her nature make laws for these hinterlands that are too easily broken.

I once thought of Cape Cod as the X-Men character of landmasses, one with unexpected and preternatural powers that would be envied round the world. But this was only my young imagination—anxiously stimulated in the era of Katrina and the Indonesian tsunami—fortifying a defensive moat around my home. I assumed we were water-repellant, and my dreams made sand strong against oceanic threats.

Recently I have been able to reteach myself about our sediment situation. It turns out that Cape Cod isn't a burly pile of wet sand, but a delicate swipe of sediment. Although flooding is not a threat, erosion is. Erosion is our blessing and our curse. This place is like a starlet with endless costume changes, massaged every year by the ocean into a new form. This place is also like a starlet in its vulnerability: so public, so beloved, and so easily shaken. Without the right protections (ecological and mental) we might spiral out of control, or melt out of existence.

An honest two-hour drive from Boston, the Outer Cape remains (for all practical purposes) pinned tight to the Eastern Seaboard. And yet our station feels removed. The arch of this isthmus swoops precariously away from North America, reaching for Atlantic isolation. Out here in the ocean, we fall under endless casts of the "painters' light." The artists and the poets come here for the atmosphere of shades.

The piping plover, our bird of place, is also known for its fragility. A hoppy little thing, it has a plump white body, and long, spindly yellow legs that move like the cartoon Roadrunner. It's a shorebird—the rarest breeding in North America—so its wings function to move it back and forth between the Gulf of Mexico and the Northeast every year. And yet those wings tuck back so neatly and tightly onto the bird's torso that you don't easily notice them. When you catch a glimpse of plovers, zipping like pinballs up and back from the break to the high-tide mark, they look less like birds and more like magical bugs or white rodents. I think their triangular bird feet were included as a decorative bonus; the marching lines of footprints they leave on the wet sand look like the petroglyphs of ancient paths—etchings rather than tracks.

Plovers are endemic to our outer lands. They make their habitat on barrier beaches, homesteading slow quicksand. We get them up on Cape Cod and others get them down along the Gulf. Their small size is not all that makes them fragile; thanks to the nature of their preferred habitats, piping plovers are vulnerable birds. In this unselfconscious insecurity, they are just like our landmass.

In 2010, conservationists and citizen ornithologists—the people who worry most about the plovers—had their concerns confirmed by national news: the birds' winter hideaways would be among the first areas to get sloshed with oil from the Deepwater Horizon spill. Being small, flighty, and not entirely photogenic, these birds were not scooped up and scrubbed clean by the people in orange gloves. (At least I didn't see them next to the shit-brown pelicans in any of the Dawn soap commercials.) Thus, the already threatened plovers became even more vulnerable. The National Audubon Society and the Cape Cod National Seashore started to whir their conservation gears. The birds that made it back up to the Outer Cape deserved safe harbor. In order to ensure this, the conservation organizations had to amp up defenses, and so the war for habitat ratcheted up a notch.

This war is being fought on the same ground where Mary Oliver walked her dog, where the blond Kennedy babies played, where Stanley Kunitz stroked his tomatoes, and where Tennessee Williams, Jackson Pollock, and Norman Mailer have all shacked up. Here on the peninsula, there are a number of war zones where we could drop in for a visit: shark vs. surfer, lobster fishermen vs. Coast Guard, popular clam shack and mini-golf place vs. start-up clam shack without mini-golf, or the never-ceasing battle that today carves the peninsula—ocean vs. dune. There is clearly a lot of fighting going on, but I don't find that unique to this region. This particular war, ongoing since 2010, appears to be between the protectors of the piping plover and some motorheads.

The plovers and the people of the Outer Cape are vying for space in a very particular environment. Out here is where land use bottlenecks. Down near Duxbury, where the Cape's arm flattens into the shoulder of Massachusetts, there is more beach and road for everyone, but less so for the towns up on the skinny wrist.

I have been spared from seeing anyone spear a plover onto a clambake kebab, because thankfully this war crops up more in township rhetoric than anywhere on the beaches. Newspapers and town hall meetings aside, bumper stickers provide the most interesting public forum. The banner representing pickups, Humvees, and Expeditions reads:

"PLOVER TASTES LIKE CHICKEN!"

The one representing Subarus and rusty two-seater Saabs:

"SAVE THE PLOVER!"

These two statements challenge each other in passing on Route 6 or when jammed up in 4 P.M. close quarters on Commercial Street.

On the physical side of conflict, the beach is quite an ironic battlefield. There are nests in the trenches! In reality, these are just tire tracks in the sand, fat rivets that invite shorebirds to inhabit. Unlike footprints, these indentations made by cars don't shimmy away in a day, but stay packed down. Hollows in the sand, they provide small straight angles for plovers to dig and rub and peck straw into. Best of all, when a mama plover sits in her nest, built within a tire track, you can't see her. Neither can golden retrievers or the balding gulls. A plover can unbury her little head when she wants to check out the scene. She inches to the left: twitch, twitch, twitch. And to the right: twitch, twitch. Crouch and scoop, back down below the horizon line.

Thanks to the unexpectedly fervent presence of the Seashore and the Society, the plovers aren't losing this war, and they aren't winning it either. They get nothing but bad press, but they are making strides. All the beach closures prove it. All the closed beaches are why the people are so mad.

The Seashore and the Audubon monitor the outer beaches year-round. The government-issued signs with diagrams about the specialness of the plover stay up during all months. For most of the fall, there are skimpy plastic wire and wooden pole barricades erected around the nesting habitat. The plastic is flimsy, and the poles wave around in the wind, sticking out of the sand at slanted angles. These are the casual, off-season defenses. Besides, far fewer people drive on the beach in the off months. And the dove-haired ladies who walk their dogs cling-wrapped in windbreakers wouldn't dare let Spot get a bite at birdy.

In the spring and summer, things start to amp up. Instead of wistful wiring and limp chopstick poles, the monitors bring out their big guns. Neon orange plastic netting gets stretched between real plywood stakes. Extra "WARNING: Endangered Species Habitat" signs go up, laminated twice over and nailed onto the wood. Kids too young to sport full mustaches don the taupe-and-green canvas uniforms of the Seashore and appear everywhere with clipboards. They trudge through the sand and scribble things down, squinting and sweating in the June sun. Their broad brown hats don't do much to protect them.

Once upon a time, another man, probably also wearing some kind of canvas outfit, walked these outer beaches. He, too, was armed, perhaps not with a clipboard, but surely with a regal squint and attentive curiosity. Henry David Thoreau came here to try out travel writing. The folks at the Goldenrod Foundation (a nonprofit similar to Audubon) invoked Thoreau as the first person to draw public attention to the plover back in 1865. He even wrote in *Cape Cod* that the plover alone symbolized the outer beach: "If I were required to name a sound, the remembrance of which most perfectly revives the impression which the beach has made, it would be the . . . peep of the plover." Goldenrod is still calling public attention to the peeping one, an umbrella species: Save the plover, save the beaches! But what good are saved beaches that don't allow off-road vehicles?

If there were a mechanical ocean made of car parts, greased gears, and metal crab arms like the ones wielded by aliens in District 9, the sound of those waves crashing would be the sound of an oncoming ORV.

ORV "enthusiasts," as they are termed, take their SUVs, dune-buggy jeeps, and sometimes their four-wheelers out onto the outer beaches. Those who go in SUVs bring tents, grills, fishing poles, and large speakers. They move in to the beach, tailgating daringly close to the breakwater. People on four-wheelers and in buggies don't go out and stay, they just charge out on joyrides, fresh from a boozy P-Town oyster bar. Accelerators tease the slippage area along the dunes and roar through the flats at low tide.

The National Seashore charges a high price for off-road permits, as it does for fire pits and nonresidential beach stickers. So these enthusiasts are recreators but certainly not casual ones. They pay up and plan ahead for their chance to unleash their engines on the sand. But releasing giddy petrol power on the sand also means unleashing doom upon the nesting plover.

In high summer when the beaches are sporadically closed to ORVs, these folks feel cheated. Another uncomfortable effect of seasonal land use bottleneck: the birds and the drivers and the locals and the out-of-towners all want the sand at the same time. It's troubling to decide who "deserves" the beach.

After 2010, the Seashore started closing beaches entirely and no one, and no thing, was allowed any access. Full-blown beach closures have occurred since 1986 whenever many flocks of plovers end up nesting in close proximity on one beach. In 2010, however, the Seashore started closing the same beaches repeatedly. They hoped that giving the plovers back their uninterrupted habitat for a few days a week would ensure that a few couples nested success-fully. They imagined they were stabilizing the population that had suffered such losses in the Gulf; they would close and block off a different beach for three to four days each week, and all of a sudden the birds would have their habitat back. But in the human realm, no one got a price deduction on permits or parking stickers. The enthusi-asts became the enraged. If you're pro-vehicle, you aren't enthused about the little lives that roll away in the wakes of your displaced sands. Hard metal and stench, gas and gears have already gotten you going. I believe these people need a reorientation of the senses. Getting acquainted with the plover might just slice open the suture binding them to mechanical mentalities. I believe this bird can teach us how to move.

The shore is silent. The sun is a tuning fork: reeds, wind, and wave make one clarifying hum. The sand is warm, magnetically warm. It calls to you like your unmade bed does in those first five minutes after waking.

Everything is moving slightly. You dig your foot into the sand and it rolls away, luxurious. When the wind makes off with the sand on an upswing breeze it titters away, seeming less like particulate and more like a strip of silk. The waves move like molasses. Slow bass drums.

Down by the water's edge, cotton balls whiz around, moving in call-and-response with the petite bayside waves. No, not cotton balls: birds. Plovers, doing their running dance, buffering the break. The sensuality of slight.

Artists come to Cape Cod to work, and sometimes to live. The light and the daring feeling they get from living on a precipice heighten their receptivity. As Stanley Kunitz said: the blue out here is bluer. The "brine-spiked" air is what we're snorting.

> Oh, to love what is lovely, and will not last!
> What a task
> to ask
> of anything or anyone,
> yet it is ours,
> and not by the century or the year, but by the
>   hours.

Mary Oliver, who lives in Provincetown, wrote that in her poem "Snow Geese." She writes things like that in many of her poems. The Cape, our common teacher, instructs us about impermanence. Of course there is a lot of Eastern religious philosophy behind the curtain, too, but there's a reason she came to the Outer Cape to practice. It's easy to find presence in passing here.

If we want to be visceral Cape Codders, we ought to locate ourselves in this state of passing. I know that we cannot fully understand where we are unless we internalize a piece of our surroundings. In June you will find me lying on the sand, a piece of straw in my teeth. I will draw in the sun that perforates my cells and run to greet the Gulf Stream as it comes to carry us away. Through these exercises, I will prostrate myself in the style of the plover.

So Cape Cod is special for artists and ORV enthusiasts. By this logic, is the National Seashore nothing more than a welcome mat?

Activities like off-roading and tailgating are ontologically opposed to life on the Outer Cape. But the life of receptivity, of sensual fragility, is for more than just the artist contingent.

I know that the ORV cadres revere the outer beaches. When I think about them I imagine a male, employed by the seasonal economy. After forty hours a week slinging shellfish on the fryers, or manning the bar at The Beachcomber, he takes to the shore to slip off the harness. He and his get their kicks from the shore just like I do. There is some element out there they also need. But perhaps they don't revere this place enough. Off-road vehicles exacerbate erosion. You don't shit where you eat. I want them to practice reverence differently. Our swipe of sediment, hanging just so before the onslaught of the Atlantic, can't accommodate everyone's idea of fun.

In order to love and live with what can't last, we need to get oriented with vulnerability, and we need to move with gentleness. When you walk down those old and greening wooden stairs, you don't slam your heels. Let's take that atmospheric injection from the Outer Cape entirely into our bloodstream. Our endemic species, the umbrella bird, can be our choreographer. Levitate, oscillate, and twitch. Do not rev.

Why I Wear Jordans
in the Great Outdoors

CJ Goulding

I am an African American natural leader. That phrase is
not an oxymoron, but it's also not something that you normally see in the environmental world.

In the few years that I have been involved in environmental education and connecting people with outdoor
spaces, there have been numerous occasions where I am the
only person of color in the program, or the only African
American leader. Growing up, there was no one from my
neighborhood traveling, hiking, canoeing, or spending time
outdoors unless it was a part of a regimented program.

But do not misunderstand the meaning behind that
statement; do not miss my point.

I write, neither to complain that the outdoor world is an
elitist one, nor to lament the disconnect between the world
I grew up in and the natural world where I now lay roots.

I write to celebrate the amazing opportunity available for me (and others like myself) to be a bridge between the two worlds.

On my feet as I write are Jordan Bred 11s, the only pair of Michael Jordan's brand of sneakers I have ever owned in my life. His sneakers are a status symbol in the neighborhood I grew up in, a memento of importance and significance. Unfortunately, for some people, they hold higher value than food, books, rent, and, in some extreme cases, even the life and well-being of another individual.

So it makes sense that while I was facilitating an outdoor youth summit last June at Harpers Ferry National Historical Park in West Virginia, an African American teenage boy stopped me to ask why I was wearing these Bred 11s outdoors. I laughed, because that same question and all the underlying ones that accompanied it had been asked of me multiple times that week, and my introspective journey in figuring out that answer led me to write this story.

In response, I asked him if he had ever seen someone from the "outdoor world" wearing Jordans. His answer was no.

I asked him if he had seen anyone who would wear Jordans exploring the outdoors like we were. Again his answer was no.

The disconnect between the two circles was evident, and as we looked around, we could see that even there, we were in the minority.

And with that same mind-set, I used to believe that I stood on a decrepit bridge between two worlds.

I have heard the rallying cry echo through the trees, affirming that the outdoors is for people of all creeds, countries, and colors. I have been a part of programs that aim to introduce these natural spaces to kids from the inner city who don't have the awareness, opportunity, or means to go camping or hiking every weekend.

I have heard the questions posed every time I prepare to travel to a "wild place" away from home, and have seen the confusion that arises when my family attempts to describe what I do.

But two summers ago, in the infancy of my outdoor career, while serving as a trip leader for the North Cascades Institute, the seed of connection between the two seemingly mutually exclusive circles was planted. For that summer, I was the only male African American leader, and I quickly learned the importance of setting an example. During that time, I had many conversations with the teenagers on my trips about where I came from, what I was doing out in nature, and why I chose to do it.

That summer, I learned the nuances of nature and the outdoors right alongside my kids, and nature taught us all about the power of perseverance through struggles with camping equipment, long canoe paddles, and strenuous hikes. And although I had taken notice of the difference between where I was at that moment and where I grew up, the seed of connection between the two worlds took root and grew without any intentional nurturing from me.

Eventually it came to my conscious attention through

one of the teenagers on my trip, a boy who, as we were preparing to separate on our last day, said that although he was hesitant at first, he now enjoyed being outdoors in nature "because CJ did." And I realized the tremendous impact that I could have.

I no longer saw the singularity of my skin tone among my peers as a problem, but instead as a megaphone to give weight to the message that as people of color, people from different ethnic backgrounds, the outdoor world is ours to explore as well. And through us, for those who had grown up connected to and educated in the outdoors, we offer the chance to connect to new cultures, to see flora and fauna through the eyes of city kids and people from different backgrounds.

Along this journey, I have met several other natural leaders of different ethnicities doing similar and amazing work, both in the inner city and out in parks and natural spaces around the country. I had the opportunity to attend the 2013 Natural Leaders Legacy Camp, an event of the national Children & Nature Network, where I connected with fifty other leaders with similar mind-sets, strengthening my resolve knowing I am not the only one out there.

My Jordans are falling apart, worn out from adventures in places like the Grand Tetons and the Grand Canyon. This goes directly against how people "should" wear them and what people "should" wear outdoors. But I wear them wherever I go to remind me of the fact that though there are two worlds, I am a bridge. In our current society, youth as a whole do not spend significant time outdoors. Yet I am encouraged by the realization of my special connecting role. And I know its importance whenever I see yet another kid from the inner city follow the footprints of my Bred 11s into the woods.

We Are the Fossil-Fuel
Freedom Fighters

Bonnie Frye Hemphill

Everything and nothing about the planet has changed in my lifetime. I am twenty-seven. Everything, because I have never known a time when our home didn't have a man-made fever. And nothing, because we've done so little to stop stoking it. "Global warming is all we've ever known," Ben Lowe, a founder of Young Evangelicals for Climate Action, explained to the *Wall Street Journal*. This conundrum makes Bill McKibben's 1989 book, *The End of Nature*, into Cassandra in a time capsule: prescient, ignored, and almost buried.

But only "almost." In the past decade, hundreds of thousands of Americans (and millions of people worldwide) have taken part in a social movement for climate solutions. Folks are marching from all walks of life: grandparents and students, businesspeople and people of faith, farmers and veterans, health advocates and parents. People are organizing local food co-ops and carpools, and developing wind farms in their towns for clean energy and greater local tax revenues. Voters are approving municipal bonds to build better transit systems, and they're petitioning legislators for renewable energy policies. They are lobbying Congress to price climate pollution, and are marching on the White House to stop the Keystone XL tar sands pipeline.

For those of us who have come of age "after the end of nature," we march with our unique means and dreams for a safer world in the face of global warming.

People used to take security in the way things were because the world seemed too big and too old to change. It seemed impossible that people could pave the prairies, mow full forests, or strip-mine the seas of protein. We could never exhaust the Earth's supply of compacted fossil life to fill our gas tanks. And never could we belch so much gas that we'd suffocate under the planet's safety blanket, choking our cool atmosphere with heat-trapping gases. Never could mere mortals call forth the seas to rise against our own cities, or hold off the rain clouds that quench our own crops, or deluge our own homes with bidden storms. The world was too big and old; we were too small and soft. So surely the way things were would be the way they'd always be.

But now all these impossibilities are terribly real. We've changed the climate, and as we feel our home failing, we're realizing that the Earth is not as big in size as it is in importance. There is no Planet B; Earth is too big to fail.

Or at any rate, it's too important that it not fail if we're to continue on a home we recognize.

Winners and losers are becoming starker as the planet fails. Monsoons fail and food prices soar in Southeast Asia. Summer rains fail in North America, congressional coffers run dry from subsidy payouts, and the Mississippi sinks too low to ship what grain survived the season. Fires char Australia and force a family under a dock. Sub-Saharan parents must work even harder to pull viable crops from desertifying fields. Superstorm Sandy decimates bankers, Brooklynites, and boardwalk roller coasters all at once. Canadian kids hear fond stories of pond hockey, but get few fond memories of their own. Again and again, Joplin, Missouri, and other towns hear tornado sirens as more powerful thunderstorms spawn more twisters. Bangladeshis, Floridians, Maldivians, and Pakistanis wade through their neighborhoods to reach higher grounds where they are not wanted. Where resources are already marginal, refugee camps are growing, and conflicts like those in Darfur and Somalia are edging further from control. As the planet's oil supply drains, American troops are in ever more danger patrolling Middle East supply lines. These are all victims of climate change, and their suffering is unjust. They—we—have the most to lose.

But walking through the Doha Exhibition Center last December, that's not who you'd think had the most to lose from a destabilizing global atmosphere. I was there in Qatar for the United Nations' annual Framework Convention on Climate Change. For nearly two decades, the world has gathered to hammer out climate solutions in a new city each year, and while the process is painfully slow—and may never succeed—at least it publicly applauds leaders and shames laggards. Taking a break from the frenetic convention, I strolled through the nearby Doha Exhibition Center to check out the booths set up by visiting institutions.

The Doha Exhibition Center is 3.7 acres of concrete and fluorescent light. Stretching over most of the acreage were exhibits for the world's largest oil companies and sovereign oil states. Saudi Aramco had turrets with plush-carpeted aeries to recline and watch PR videos. The Exxon and Chevron pavilions gleamed bleachily. BP had pastel graphics.

And yet in none of these vast exhibits was another soul visiting with me. All the other tourists were in the corner enjoying lively cubby-booths of clean-tech inventors, urban-agriculture advocates, and aggressively friendly vegans passing out cupcakes. You can guess how I felt struck by these companies' investments in empty monuments to the golden age of fossil hegemony. But hey, it makes sense: these guys have the most to lose if we build a cleaner way of life.

I left the exhibition center with losers and winners on my mind. Who has the most to lose from climate instability, and the most to gain from a cleaner, more durable, more equitably prosperous world? All of us who aren't fossil-fuel corporate executives, that's who. So who is most desperately denying us progress toward that better world? Who's polluting our landscape, our politics, and our airwaves? You guessed it. The kingpins of "clean coal," the oil barons, the fossil-fuel fat cats. My generation is fighting for climate justice, for freedom from fossil fuels.

Climate change is a problem of tremendous scale in geography—it's *global* warming—and time, as today's pollution locks us into warming a hundred years from now. The size of solutions varies wildly, too, from changing light bulbs to international treaties. And at the root of it all, the people causing climate change are very different in scale from those actively impeding solutions.

The people causing climate change are all of us. In fact, as a middle-class North American, the amount of carbon pollution I put into the atmosphere is an order of magnitude greater than that of my peers in rural India. Even as I'm "thinking green" 24/7, I still enjoy chicken, and I drive my gas-powered car to the grocery store that sells it. I flip on the heat when it's cold. And shoot, I flew across the world for a conference on climate change.

And there are millions like me, belching a lot of carbon even as we work flat-out for a better world. It's not that I want no one to drive; it's that I want new options other than oil for getting around. And it's not that I want us to live in the dark; it's that I want my electricity to come from durable sources. I want the choice to be able to live well without compromising my kids' ability to live well someday, too. My generation knows we contribute to climate instability, but that's exactly why we're working so hard to solve it. It's satisfying to be part of something hopeful and necessary. It's satisfying to be actively freeing our communities from fossil fuels.

But I'm small potatoes. There are people an order of magnitude guiltier than I for climate injustice: those who see that their profitable pasts are over. Fossil magnates are terrified of a cleaner economy. To hang on a little longer, they have spent billions of dollars in recent decades to confuse the public about the danger of climate disruption. They've paid off fake researchers to say that energy has "always" come from coal so could never come from the sun. They've set up talking heads on news channels bought and paid for, to remind people how much we like traffic jams to prevent us from voting for faster trains. They've won politicians' allegiance with campaign donations in return for ever more oil subsidies from taxpayer dollars. These fossil-fuel fat cats are poisoning our planet and our democracy's ability to solve it. They are the real culprits of climate change.

Fossil fuel companies from BP (Gulf oil spill) to TransCanada (tar sands) to Massey Energy (Big Branch mine explosion) to natural gas (fracking Pennsylvania's groundwater) have everything to lose if we innovate in safer, cleaner energy. Wind power, solar, a more efficient electrical grid, better public transit systems, more vibrant food systems independent from fossil-based fertilizers—all of these make energy safer and cheaper for us in the long term. So the fossil-fuel fat cats are proportionately petrified.

In politics, an industry with everything to lose cannot be trusted. Do you believe anything Marlboro says about lung health? No, you're much smarter than that. Anything the fossil fuel industry says on climate change or clean energy is said in fear and desperation, and those bleached booths in Doha talking up "clean coal" only prove it all the more. Sure, the climate truth hurts—it hurts a whole lot to realize we've broken our planet—but the truth is better than fossil-fuel fat cats feeding us comforting lies. But they'll feed us all they can, because people who know the truth begin to fight back.

I'm angry—can you tell? I'm angry at the insider energy powers for spending so much to derail a safe future for my generation. Their calculated denial of climate disruption earns them a place right next to those denying the Holocaust. Slow genocide or fast, it's just as cruel.

But there is nothing so powerful as self-righteous anger, and millions of us are marching on it. My grandmothers have told me stories of the World War II years, when Americans knew they had to work together and hard, because justice was not a given. My parents' generation then fought for social and environmental action, but they thought they could fully succeed—their signs said "Save the Earth" because they thought they could. Like my grandmothers, we twenty-somethings don't assume climate justice will be done; we know that we must work for it. But unlike our parents, we who have come of age after the end of nature have grown past that naïveté about the planet's durability. We know we cannot stop the climate from destabilizing.

My parents used to introduce me to their friends by offering with pride that I wanted to "save the world." My gut clenched every time, because I'm not that dumb. I have no illusions that we'll save the planet from the fossil-fueled binge of recent centuries. The planet we evolved on is over; we're now locked into the crazy weather that's on the news every night. But we can prevent collapse. We can protect our home enough to protect the human lives and livelihoods that depend on it. It's too late to save the polar bears, but it's not quite too late to save ourselves.

And in seeking that salvation, we might end up building something better than the status quo. After all, we're aiming for an economy powered by energy that doesn't blow up, innovations that require tons of new jobs, and a democracy disinfected from the desperate campaign donations of fossil-fuel fat cats afraid of the future.

My generation is hopeful, practical, strategic, and muscular—and not naïve. In fact, we are staking our very sense of self on it; we want history to write us as the ones who got to work. We are the fossil-fuel freedom fighters, and we're on the move.

More and more young people around the world are raising their communities' voices for climate solutions. In the United States, we're shutting down proposed fossil-fuel infrastructure that would lock in decades more dependence. We're hosting press conferences and town hall meetings, commissioning economists, consulting tribal elders, and publishing op-eds with medical professionals. We're lying down on the train tracks to coal export facilities proposed in the Northwest and the Gulf Coast, and we're chaining ourselves to the White House fence to demand that President Obama decline the Keystone XL tar sands pipeline. Yes, we're radical: our lives and our livelihoods depend upon it.

And thousands of students are mobilizing to press our university endowments to divest of fossil fuels. We believe that in graduating the world's next generation of leaders, universities should not simultaneously profit from the pollution that destabilizes the world we graduate into. Our means is divestment not because we can impoverish Exxon, but to send the message that fossil fuels have lost their social license. Hundreds of campuses are working to divest, joined by houses of worship, city budgets, and more.

And a new generation of entrepreneurs is starting companies in practical, profitable climate solutions. Business is booming in energy efficiency, more affordable fossil-free food, electric car-charging stations, and smarter buildings. And besides doing well for themselves by doing some good for all of us, these industries are hiring.

We proudly think of these jobs as work that needs doing, compared to the few gigs on offer from extractive industries. Those are mature industries; they do most of their mining and drilling with machines, so very few people get a career from each additional project toasting the planet. "You can create a lot of jobs drilling holes in a ship," said one retiree against the coal-export facilities proposed for his home in Bellingham, Washington. "But the ship will still go down."

By contrast, we're taking pride in careers that power us past fossil fuels. Clean-economy technologies are too new to be so mechanized; they require real skills from real people. From solar engineers to electric-car mechanics and home-weatherization experts, many of these are jobs that can't be outsourced. And this work builds a cleaner world for all of us; it's work that people are proud to do because it's work that needs doing.

Instead of trying to "save the world," my generation is building the new institutions and industries that will support a just and resilient world. We're changing systems, we're changing rules, and we're hiring.

We who have come of age after the end of nature know that we have inherited damaged goods. But we're strong and we're smart, and we can and we will rebuild.

And most importantly, we have found our very calling in doing so. We are the cool kids; "we were created to be awesome," says Kid President. We are the ones building past the assumptions handed to us, the ones building a safer, more equitable, more durable world. We are the fossil-fuel freedom fighters.

And you're invited. Will you join?

The Wager for Rain

Megan Kimble

We rolled around the shallows of Lake Michigan like beached whales, my sister and I. As a six-year-old, I couldn't see land on the other side, but the water didn't make my lips crinkle or taste like salt. "It's a lake," my parents said. "Who made it?" I asked. "No one," they said. It just was. The next summer, back home in California, we waded into the icy, mulch-covered shoreline of Big Bear Lake. This seemed like a lake, too, but then my dad clarified: someone had made this lake. Big Bear Lake was a reservoir, Bear Creek trans-formed, the accumulation of a once-flowing river halted by a cement dam and corralled into a natural canyon. A few winters later, during Christmas break, my family and I drove north from Los Angeles to Mammoth Mountain, a six-hour drive that crossed over the great cement river of the California aqueduct. We crammed our feet into ski boots and trundled to the lifts, poles flailing. It had been a mild winter so the slopes were manned by great rumbling machines—they looked like giant hair-dryers pointed skyward—that spewed white flakes across the groomed hills. My sister, ten years old and annoyed by the rumbling, informed us that she did not like the fake snow.

I didn't get it. How was fake snow different from real snow? They were both cold and white and melted on my nose. How was a constructed lake different from a natural lake? They were both holes in the ground filled with water.

When I returned to my fifth-grade classroom, I learned about the water cycle in a classroom full of glitter- and glue-covered poster boards. Arrows of water burst out of cotton ball clouds, sped toward the earth in tight fists of rain, lingered on green blades of grass in wavering dewdrops, and finally shimmied upward again; the drops evaporated into the atmosphere and eventually returned home to the cloud. Condensation, evaporation, precipitation. The litany reminds us that the water exists in three states— solid, liquid, gas—and that even if we can't see it, water is all around us.

By the time I got to high school, my vocabulary acquired enough nuance—reclamation, aqueduct, ice crystal—that I began to understand the distinctions among types of lakes—types of rivers, types of snow—as one of genesis rather than function. Humans dammed up fake lakes and machines spewed fake snow. Nature made natural lakes and real snow. The classifying language of science claimed to resolve the distinction between human-made and natural forms of water, and indeed, it seemed resolved for me until I returned to the lesson of that fifth-grade classroom and began to think less about the receptacle of water than the water itself, part of a dynamic and cycling existence.

Water was water—two hydrogen atoms and one oxygen atom—wherever it happened to appear, be it lake or stream, aqueduct or reservoir, snow-machine or summer monsoon. Did it lose its identity according to what force had shaped it? If engineers could corral these water molecules into a lake, if they could freeze them into snow to dust over a mountaintop . . . could they just make water appear wherever they wanted to? Was there such a thing as manufactured rain?

Clouds form when water vapor in the air condenses into liquid water droplets. How or when water vapor condenses into droplets depends on air pressure and temperature and particulates in the air. Hot things expand and cool ones contract. Air near the hot earth rises, expanding toward the sky. Similarly, liquid water molecules simmering on the surface of a lake heat up, transform into vapor, and expand skyward, escaping unseen from their source. Thus freed, they latch onto the nitrogen and carbon molecules of the air. But as the once-expansive hot air—that air that had welcomed those adventure-seeking water molecules—reaches the cooler stratosphere, it contracts. Colder and denser, the air no longer can hold onto all the water vapor molecules that had climbed aboard back down on earth. The air becomes saturated, and the water molecules must find a new host.

That host is called a condensation nucleus. If the air were perfectly clean, clouds wouldn't form; humidity would float in nebulous streams across the landscape. But the air isn't clean; it is full of dust, salt, pollutants, and particles of ice that serve as gathering points for these wandering water molecules. Water molecules—still in their gaseous state—condense around these nuclei. After enough molecules gather, vapor becomes liquid. A droplet forms. More molecules gather. As molecules gather, the droplet gets heavier and heavier. Finally, finally . . . it falls.

The most common naturally occurring condensation nuclei are ice crystals. The supply of ice crystals, however, is limited by humidity and temperature. Lacking condensation nuclei, water wanders vaporously throughout the atmosphere. Even as swaths of the earth below cry out for rain, without condensation nuclei there is nothing for water to do but wander and wait, wait until a burst of dust or a high-atmospheric freeze sweeps the seeds of rain across the sky. For centuries, humans also simply waited. They waited for the condensation nuclei to arrive, for water molecules to crowd around these nuclei, for a drop to become—slowly, gradually—heavy enough to fall.

Growing up in Los Angeles, beholden to the man-made lakes and rivers of the West, I didn't realize that I lived in a desert. From what I could see, I lived on Hillard Avenue. Though the Santa Ana winds occasionally whipped dust through our backyard, mostly I sat in the backseat of the family Volvo as my mom drove along cement corridors to air-conditioned grocery stores. I turned on the faucet and water came out—why wouldn't it? Water was as inevitable as sunshine. My complacency was the complacency of Los Angeles, the city built on possibility and the expectation that the Colorado River would forever irrigate its palm trees. I only began to question this when I left California and went next door, to Arizona—California's water rival.

I moved to Tucson, a scrappy cactus-adorned city plunked in the middle of the Sonoran Desert. Dwellings in Tucson do not congeal into contiguous human settlement; they are concrete islands in a desert sea of mesquite and brush and tumbleweeds. Now, I run along dry riverbeds and swelter under the sun, and I begin to see, finally, the tenuous infrastructure that siphons water into my tap. How, before humans wrestled the desert into an uneasy submission, could this place have sustained life? Tucson is one of the oldest continually inhabited human settlements in North America—ceramic artifacts uncovered by archeologists suggest humans settled here more than 12,000 years ago. It is unbelievable to consider, yet populations of early inhabitants were sparse—and they had their rivers. The Santa Cruz, the Rillito, the Gila. Once seasonally flowing rivers, they are now only memories, dirt canyons that harden in the winters and flood effluent during summer monsoons.

There are no running rivers and it never seems to rain, yet my toilet always flushes and my faucet always runs. Seven inches of annual rainfall, and there are a million of us in Tucson alone, flushing toilets and running faucets. But here, unlike in Los Angeles, the anxiety about all these flushing toilets and running faucets is palpable. Arizona has pumped more water out of the ground in the past eighty years than it will in the next thousand—like fossil fuel, groundwater is a finite resource—and the Central Arizona Project, southern Arizona's 340-mile lifeline to the Colorado River, has been built. There's no more water coming down the pipe. We huddle on our desert island, clinging to the cement lifeline snaking across the state, and wonder—I wonder, at least—what happens next.

On a Monday morning in September, I am reading the "Layperson's Guide to Arizona Water" and am stopped in my tracks by the dream of cloud seeding. I am a layperson in both senses of the word—neither an ordained member of a church nor a professional academic—but I suppose that the publication's source, the University of Arizona's Water Resources Research Center, does not intend to confer religious overtones to the subject of creating water in a desert. Water officials predict a 25 percent chance that water supply won't meet demand within the next ten years, but we are reassured: "Scholars believe that when the Hohokam population grew beyond its ability to stretch its limited water supplies, the civilization failed. But these early desert dwellers lacked the technological resources of contemporary water managers, and Arizona is now developing new ways to manage and extend this scarce resource." I scrawl in the margin: "But this won't happen to us, technology will save us!" I realize it is the resources of contemporary water managers that allow water to flow freely out of my faucets, but alone in my apartment, it is too easy to criticize human hubris. "One technology is cloud seeding. Cloud seeding injects chemicals such as silver iodide into clouds to allow water droplets or ice crystals to form more easily, increasing precipitation." I have never heard of cloud seeding and I am scandalized—or entranced—by the idea. It's as if I were not the only wide-eyed seven-year-old who believed in the possibility of man-made rain. I scribble: "layperson's guide?!"

In July 1946, at General Electric's laboratory in Schenectady, New York, chemist Vincent Schaefer was fiddling with supercooled clouds. But it was July and his cloud chamber was too hot. The clouds refused to be supercooled. Frustrated, he tossed a chunk of solid carbon dioxide—dry ice—into the humid chamber to cool it down. It was like throwing fish food into a pond. Immediately, water molecules rushed around the newly introduced ice crystals and clouds formed where there had been only humid air. Meanwhile, atmospheric scientist Bernard Vonnegut—the novelist Kurt's brother—was tinkering with silver and iodine and realized that silver iodide had the same lattice structure as ice and thus would have the same effect as ice crystals in clouds. In other words, scientists now had the means to introduce condensation nuclei into clouds, providing a gathering point for water molecules floating aimlessly in the air. Within just a few weeks, scientists suddenly knew how to stop waiting and start raining. Ice crystals—or their chemical counterparts—are the seeds of rain. Plant the seed and, according to laboratory logic, rain should grow.

Five months after Schaefer chucked dry ice into a cloud chamber and changed atmospheric science, he attempted his first cloud-seeding experiment. He dumped six pounds of dry ice into a cloud near Mount Greylock in western Massachusetts. It snowed.

Though cloud seeding has been appropriated by academics at the University of Arizona and elsewhere, it's hardly the first attempt to stir up rain in the desert. Cloud seeding is technological rainmaking. Starting with the first people who settled here, the Hohokam, indigenous civilizations have practiced elaborate ceremonies to entice the rain from the clouds. We may well dismiss their rainmaking as the religion of a failed civilization, but the Tohono O'odham, another people who have lived on the desert land for centuries, are very much still alive and flourishing, and continue to perform rainmaking ceremonies every year—music, cactus wine, and dancing are the seeds to their clouds. Maybe I am stopped in my tracks on a Monday morning because, contained within this layperson's guide, cloud seeding feels no less religious to me than a rain dance.

Beginning nearly a century before Schaefer and Vonnegut's big breakthroughs, according to climate historian James Rodger Fleming in *Fixing the Sky*, the U.S. government had already been spending millions of dollars trying to make it rain. James Espy, who worked as National Meteorologist for the U.S. Army Medical Department in the 1840s, proposed burning thousands of acres of Rocky Mountain forest in order to initiate rainfall on the Great Plains. In the last half of the nineteenth century, despite the wry assurances by University of Texas professor Alexander Macfarlane "that it is impossible to produce rain by making a great noise," "rainmaking by concussion" enjoyed its heyday in budget allocations and scholarly studies. In 1891, the U.S. government offered a grant to Robert St. George Dyrenforth, a patent lawyer from D.C., to study if a great racket could indeed shake the drops from the sky. Dyrenforth arrived in El Paso, Texas, in August with a battalion of mortars, dynamite, and smoke bombs, and began firing at the clouds. The Secretary of Agriculture came out for a demonstration. "The result," he said, "was a loud noise!" Well after cloud seeding had gone mainstream, in 1963, James Black and Barry Tarmy, two employees of the Esso Research and Engineering Company, published a paper asserting that "useful amounts of rainfall might be produced" by "coating a large area with asphalt." The promise of the Homestead Act—rain follows plow— had come of age. Now, it seemed, rain follows asphalt. By the 1970s, the federal government was spending $20 million a year on weather-modification programs.

In the 1960s and 1970s, the University of Arizona conducted a series of experiments to measure the effectiveness of cloud seeding. After two decades of research, the studies were inconclusive. Cloud seeding didn't not work, the studies said, but it didn't really work, either. Or maybe it did, but if it did, it was impossible to measure. One study offered the "inescapable conclusion" that "cloud seeding in the Arizona experiment must have decreased the rainfall in those areas that were far downwind." Cloud seeding certainly did something. It was just unclear whether or not that something was rainmaking.

A scientist or farmer or ski resort operator seeds a cloud; he (it's usually a he) sends plumes of dry ice or silver iodide into the atmosphere, hoping the chemicals will prod precipitation out of dormant clouds. It rains (or it doesn't) and you can measure the rain that falls. But how do you measure the rain that didn't fall—the rain that wouldn't have fallen, the rain that couldn't have fallen save for the meddling of a savvy scientist? We seed some clouds, and some clouds rain. But we don't seed fog (because fog seeding doesn't work). We seed clouds that seem like they might rain. When the clouds that seem like they might rain do indeed rain, how do we know we had anything to do with it?

In 1995, a group led by Eric Betterton, then an atmospheric physics professor at the University of Arizona, spent two months seeding winter clouds outside Prescott and Sedona. Using radar imaging, they saw direct precipitation below a cloud immediately after seeding—proof! seeding works!—but couldn't track the precipitation down to the ground to verify that the water didn't simply evaporate back into the dry desert air. Nonproof.

Fifteen years after the last cloud-seeding study at the University of Arizona, I called Eric Betterton, who is now the head of the university's Department of Atmospheric Sciences.

"The people who say there is such a thing as cloud seeding will say that you get a 10 percent increase in precipitation, which is well within the noise of any given rainstorm," he tells me. "The problem is"—the problem of his experiment in 1995—"can you show increased precipitation on the ground?"

I ask Betterton what he means by "those who believe in such a thing as cloud seeding."

"Cloud seeding is almost like a religion," he says. "There are those who believe in that and there are those who don't. A few people sit in on the fence, but mostly those two camps won't talk to each other."

"And you?" I ask.

"I'm an agnostic," he says.

The Atmospheric Sciences Department at the University of Arizona, the department that Betterton himself heads, owes its existence to cloud seeding. Lewis Douglas, an Arizona congressman who served in Franklin Roosevelt's administration, owned a ranch share in southern Arizona, caught whiff of the silver iodide snow blowing around General Electric, and decided to direct some rain toward his ranch. And why not? He had the clout to convince the Arizona legislature to fund weather-modification research, and they kindly obliged, founding the Institute of Atmospheric Physics in 1954.

I ask Betterton about silver iodide. "Is it a cause for concern? Injecting this chemical into the atmosphere, into our water supply, our rivers, drinking water?"

"The concentrations are so low that they have no effect," he says. "They're so low that you need specialized analytical equipment just to detect it. The concentrations that appear in snow or rain are so low as to be negligible."

These days, about 50,000 kilograms of silver iodide are thrown in the air every year to seed the clouds.

Research and funding for cloud seeding peaked in the 1970s; an extra forty years of research hasn't changed the conclusion that cloud seeding may or may not work, and that it probably doesn't. In 2003, after fifty years of research in the United States, the National Research Council released a report that concluded, "There is still no convincing scientific proof of the efficacy of intentional weather-modification efforts."

We are desperate. The West needs water, and the Colorado River has never been able to live up to our expectations. In 1922, when the Colorado River Compact was signed to divvy up the water of its namesake, hydrologists measured the Colorado River at an annual flow of 16.4 million acre-feet. They weren't wrong. They had just measured the river during one of the wettest years in its history—the wettest year in at least a century. The 1922 Colorado River Compact split the river's annual flow—its mistaken flow of 16.4 million—into two theoretical halves, like a Popsicle split between bickering siblings. Half for the upper basin states—Colorado, Utah, Wyoming, and New Mexico— and half for the lower—California, Arizona, and Nevada (and the trickling leftovers went to Mexico). It was a promise no one could keep—least of all the river. Water originated in the upper basin states, yet population and agriculture demanded it in the lower. Since then, upper and lower basin states have been at odds, bickering over the two halves that are quickly evaporating into the heat. Since 1930, the Colorado River's average annual flow has been closer to 13 million acre-feet. As snowpack in the Colorado Rockies diminishes and high-pressure systems linger over the Southwest, that number threatens to dip lower. Dust storms gather like it's the 1930s, and drought wrings the desert dry.

By now we might as well insert ourselves into the water cycle, as fat raindrops fall into man's outstretched hands. Raindrops are dumped into irrigation ditches or toilet bowls, scrubbed through wastewater treatment systems, and, finally, cast back to nature, dribbling through concrete-lined rivers toward the sea. What water does escape to join the evaporation arrow—the arrow that heads back toward the clouds—is labeled a deserter, a subversive. Engineers speak of water that is "lost to evaporation," like soldiers going AWOL. But of course, water is not lost, nor is it created—there is no such thing as new water. Water simply cycles.

In the humid Midwest of my family's genesis, to waste water is to use it needlessly. In California and Arizona, "to waste water is not to consume it—to let it flow unimpeded and undiverted down rivers," wrote Marc Reisner in *Cadillac Desert*. The legacy of the half-century American dam-building bonanza is precisely this attitude: water is wasted if it returns to the sea unused. "By the late 1970s," wrote Reisner, "there were 1,251 major reservoirs in California, and every significant river—save one—had been dammed at least once." In 1901, President Roosevelt was irritated by all the undammed "waters that now run to waste" and demanded they be "saved and used for irrigation." Today's dormant rain clouds hovering over parched landscapes are yesterday's "wasted" rivers. Those subversive escapees—the water molecules lost to evaporation—taunt us from the skies. The water is there, hovering over us, vaporous and unattainable.

As the Colorado River, the lifeline that sustains twenty-five million people, threatens to wane, anything extra we can squeeze out of the clouds may seem worth its cost. For $15,000, a farmer can buy a year's supply of silver iodide and a propane-fired generator, no bigger than a snow machine, to pump it into the atmosphere. Most cloud-seeding projects begin at this scale, with small groups like municipalities or irrigation districts pooling their resources to invest in the applied science of rainmaking. Eighty percent of the West's water comes from snowpack, so snowfall augmentation programs are especially popular—and convenient—for bankrupt cities, as they're often paid for by thirsty ski resorts. Colorado, Utah, New Mexico, Nevada, California, and Wyoming have supported snowfall augmentation programs for decades. Though it is impossible to measure how much extra water reaches the Colorado River as a result of cloud seeding, that these programs survive when teachers' pensions do not suggests that someone is convinced they are working. Nevada claims a 6 to 12 percent increase in snowfall due to cloud seeding; California holds theirs is 4 percent.

Arizona is in fact the only state in the Colorado basin

not seeding its clouds. "I can't say I know why that is," said Rand Decker, a professor of civil engineering and water resources at Northern Arizona University. He's under contract by water interests in the state to facilitate conversations about cloud seeding.

I ask him how these conversations are going. "I don't harbor a strong position in respect to the activity itself," he says. "It is reasonable to assume you might get between a 0 and 11 percent increase in precipitation."

"So you might get zero?" I ask.

"Those are both end numbers of a big navy. You might get zero. But I'm not in a position to argue terms." He is hedging his words—in a world of zealots, he too is careful to appear agnostic. "You might get no return as water on your investment. What was the value then?" He pauses. "Besides injecting a few thousand dollars into a local economy."

If the saying is true, and water flows toward money, now that all the groundwater in the West has been staked and claimed, we have turned to throwing our spare change at the clouds.

It is perhaps this sense of futility that has inspired faint glimmers of cooperation. Though upper and lower basin states have been wrangling over Colorado River water for decades, Decker now tells me that "a number of wholesale water supply entities in the lower Colorado River basin"—like the Central Arizona Project—"are purchasing additional snowpack augmentation capacity in upper basin states." The logic is like six degrees of Kevin Bacon—if you seed clouds in the Rocky Mountains, there will be more snowpack, which means more snowmelt, which means that, eventually, somewhere down the line, hopefully, there will be more water in the Colorado River. "If you increase water supplies in the upper basin, it leads to increased chances of having our full water allocation of Colorado River available to us in the lower basin," says Decker.

The chances are erratic—between 0 and 11 percent. "But if you do get some more water, are you willing to take that chance . . ." He trails off.

Take that chance. We throw our money at the clouds; a few thousand dollars for the chance of rain seems like a small price to pay. Decker is paid to facilitate conversation, and conversation seeds action.

If scientists comprise the sect of the agnostics, then the Weather Modification Association—the representative of the people in the business of weather modification—is the church of the seeders. Since 1950, the consultants, scientists, engineers, and economists who comprise the Weather Modification Association have promoted the science of cloud seeding, calling the demands for proof by agnostics like Betterton so "stringent that few atmospheric problems"—like global warming—could satisfy them.

Cloud seeding is Pascal's wager: "God is, or He is not," French philosopher Blaise Pascal wrote in *Pensées*. "According to reason, you can defend neither of the propositions. . . . Let us weigh the gain and the loss in wagering that God is. . . . If you gain, you gain all; if you lose, you lose nothing." Cloud seeding is the wager for rain or the wager against rain. If the status quo is drought, why not wager, even if we still don't know exactly what happens in a cloud?

Sverre Petterssen, a prominent Norwegian meteorologist in the middle of the twentieth century, wrote, "In the atmosphere, processes of vastly different spatial scales and life spans exist together and interact; impulses and energy are shuttled throughout the whole spectrum of phenomena— all the way from molecular processes to global circulations and the changes in the atmosphere as a whole."

Atmospheric scientist William Cotton, a world-renowned expert on cloud seeding, writes, "In weather modification experiments, the scientific community requires 'proof' that cloud seeding has increased precipitation. . . . Such 'proof' would include strong physical evidence of appropriate modifications to cloud structures and highly significant statistical evidence." That he includes "proof" in quotation marks suggests he might understand there's more to be understood about a cloud than its quantifiables, yet he is right: proof is required.

A few months after I learn that cloud seeding exists, I am perusing the UA Atmospheric Sciences webpage and see that William Cotton is scheduled to give a seminar at the University of Arizona on November 17. I look at my calendar. Next Thursday.

He's a diminutive fellow, a professor emeritus at Colorado State University who slouches a bit and smiles, joking about escaping the snow of Colorado for the sunshine of Arizona. Cloud condensation nuclei (CCN), he says, "invigorate the

dynamics of convection clouds," and I picture little silver
iodide molecules wearing gym shorts and demanding that
the water droplets that went AWOL from the Colorado
River do push-ups and cartwheels to prepare to return to
their squadron. Thus invigorated, they are ready to jump.
But—always the but—"it is not necessarily the case that
increased CCN increases rainfall," says Cotton, the beam
of his laser pointer hovering over a colorful radar graph of
cloud densities and precipitation levels.

This is sixty years after Vincent and Bernard invigorated
cloud chambers at General Electric and still nobody knows
if this actually works.

What we do know is that humans affect the atmosphere,
intentionally or not. A study by Cotton and his group
proved the existence of what is known as inadvertent seeding—cloud seeding by accident. While farmers the next
state over pay thousands of dollars to inject silver iodide
into their clouds, metro-dwellers in Houston, Texas, inad-
vertently send enough particulates into the atmosphere
every day that they cloud seed by accident. Houston's pollution creates a measurable "urban plume" downwind of
the city. Particulates from this plume find their way into
clouds and, in some cases, catalyze droplet formation. In
other cases, however, aerosol pollutants have the effect of
"over-seeding" clouds, effectively suppressing precipitation.
Though the specific outcomes are still unclear—more rain
or less rain—it's clear that the stuff spewing from our
cities—from our factories and automobiles and air-conditioning—affects the clouds on a much grander scale than

whatever we dump into them on purpose. Whether we like it or not, we are seeding the clouds.

Rain dances are rituals, and rituals are more about process than result. A thirsty farmer spends $15,000 on a silver iodide machine, points it toward the forsaken sky, and feels like he is doing something. Rainmaking is an act of keeping faith, and I wonder if cloud seeding is the scientific version of this—if this is what an act of faith looks like in a technological age on a warming planet. I understand the temptation, the allure, to fix the sky—to control the uncontrollable.

But the question I expected a simple answer to has yet to be answered: Does seeding a cloud produce more rain? "To determine whether or not the atmosphere has responded to outside interference, it is necessary to predict what would have happened had it been left alone," wrote Petterssen. We cannot predict would have and could have, just as we cannot quantify the rain that doesn't hit the ground. In the words of Eric Betterton, "People have been trying [cloud seeding] a long, long time and the jury is still out." Yet a 2001 estimate by the National Oceanic and Atmospheric Administration counted sixty-six active weather modification programs across ten states.

The West needs water. We try to cut back, to be more efficient and turn off our faucets, but change is hard. Change requires patience, and cloud seeding could give us water now. Cloud seeding is less about what is than the allure of what could be. Is half an inch of rain worth it?

Maybe it doesn't work—maybe we get zero inches instead of eleven—but what if it does? What if it rains?

There may come a time when proof becomes irrelevant—when we will have to proceed through ambiguity. If it turns out that things are worse than we thought—if carbon dioxide levels reach an unforeseen tipping point, catalyzing all at once the climate changes that scientists predicted would happen gradually—we will be glad that we wagered. As Pascal wrote, "You must wager. It is not optional." Doing nothing is as much of an action as doing something. Increasingly, climate change is something everyone wagers on, even if by simply ignoring it. Just as you can't measure the rain that didn't fall—what would have happened—you can't measure what we didn't try.

We reach after fact and reason, but we linger in ambiguity. The complexity of clouds eludes prediction, escapes quantification. Water vapor swirls across the desert and settles in our eyebrows and nose hairs. We can't see it but we know that it's there. We seed the clouds and hope that it rains. In a drought, why not wager? In the end, seeded water is water just the same.

Could Mopping Save the World?

How Day-to-Day Chores Can Bring Big Changes

Emily Schosid

On the day I arrive at Lama, it takes me a few minutes to find the people. When I find them, they are holding hands around a large octagonal table, centered in the huge octagonal kitchen. They're singing a song to bless the dinner they are about to eat. A large photo of Amma, the Hugging Saint, watches from the window, her round face and wrinkled eyes smiling. The shelves around the kitchen are cluttered with idols, stones, feathers, and bowls; dried plants and pots and pans of every size and shape hang on the walls. A brown striped cat lazily surveys the room from the top of the refrigerator.

Before any words can escape my mouth, I'm bear-hugged by a tall man with a wild mane of red hair. He introduces himself as Sebastian and soon he is introducing me to everyone else seated around the table. He laughs and tells me they typically refer to themselves as "Lama Beans," all of whom file past me, hug me, and say hello. I quietly sip my soup and marvel at what one visitor to Lama later called their "expert greeting powers."

I look around suspiciously. People sprinkle things like "Bragg Liquid Aminos," "dietary yeast," and "za'atar" onto their soup. One woman animatedly recalls a conversation she recently had with the raspberry bush outside.

The only thing I can think is that this has to be some kind of cult.

The Lama Foundation is a spiritual community, educational facility, and retreat center nestled in the Sangre de Cristo Mountains of northern New Mexico. The community is open to people from all walks of life and all spiritual traditions, and believes that there are infinite ways to commune with God, Allah, cosmic energies, nature, or whatever other name one might have for the divine. Though I didn't quite understand the missions of Lama, they offer a space for people to experience living in community, working on a personal "curriculum" of self-discovery, as well as a beautiful setting for a variety of workshops and retreats. These range from a permaculture design course to youth retreats, to "vast silence," a deeply spiritual meditation retreat that is still led by Lama's cofounder, Asha Greer.

When I first learned about the Lama Foundation, they described themselves as a "sustainable, spiritual community," and I couldn't resist my curiosity to find out what that really meant and how a sustainable community actually worked. Realist and alarmist environmentalists alike have been telling us for decades that we are going to need a new way of living if we don't want to run out of clean water, clean air, or safe food. I thought Lama might have some of the answers to what that different way of living could look like. As I drove up the winding road to this idealized place, I'd imagined the solar panels, composting toilets, and rainwater collection systems that I had heard were the community's—nay, the world's—salvation. But hugging saints and liquid aminos? I had assumed that Lama would be a sustainable community that was also spiritual, but it was clear within those first few minutes after hugging Sebastian and looking around the kitchen that Lama was definitely a spiritual community before all else—something that my bare-bones religious belief, if you could call my near-atheism that, was unprepared for.

When I go to bed that first night, I'm sure I've made some kind of mistake.

During dinner that first evening, I meet Lucas, the summer intern coordinator—or, as they call him, the "steward guardian"—who offers to take me on a short tour of the grounds. Lucas shakes my hand and then pulls me into a hug. "It's so good to finally meet you after all those emails!"

As with the rest of Lama, the image I had formed of Lucas before my arrival is far from the image that stands before me. His blond hair is pulled back into a tight ponytail. He's got an eyebrow ring and the piercings in his ears hold inch-wide wooden plugs. He radiates the vibes of the rock musician he was before coming to Lama. He tells me he's been at Lama for three years, and I can tell he's been working at this spirituality thing in earnest for a long time. Lucas, like Sebastian and about eight others around the table at dinner, are the community's "residents"—people who live on the land year-round, rather than "stewards" like myself who only live on the land for a few months during the summers. After the busy summer retreat season ends, Lama empties except for the rotating group of about eight to fifteen residents, who take on more extensive spiritual practice and training, learn to be leaders in the community before the land fills with people the following summer, and keep the buildings from being taken over by mice seeking shelter from the cold mountain winter.

Lucas leads me out the back doors of the kitchen and tells me that he'll start off by taking me to the Dome, the central meeting space for the community. On our way, I spot four solar hot-water panels glistening in the late-day sun—just the stuff I was hoping to see here. I make a mental note to ask about them later. When we get to the doors of the Dome, Lucas tells me to kick off my shoes, since it is considered a "sacred space." I nod as I struggle to balance on one leg and pull my shoes off.

When we walk in the squeaky front doors, my jaw drops. I've never seen a room like this. In front of me is an enormous octagonal window. The blazing orange and pink sunset streams in, leaving the mountains to the west in stark, black silhouette. Just before the mountains, the winding Rio Grande is highlighted in yellow and brown shadows, and the falling sun has turned the clouds into swirling red ribbons across the sky.

The room is round, and the roof, as the name of the building implies, is stretched into a towering domed shape. Directly above the middle of the room is a skylight in the shape of an eight-pointed star.

Lucas explains that this is the place we will come for such things as "Practice and Tuning." I nod again, but have absolutely no idea what "Practice and Tuning" could be.

He leads me back outside and up some crudely cut stone steps, pointing out the washhouse, the greenhouses, and the rows of newly planted vegetables. Tattered and sun-faded prayer flags flap from the handmade fences that line the gardens. Lucas points out the path to the outhouse, and I make another mental note to ask about that later, too. We start down a long dirt path toward what looks like an empty campground.

We turn a corner and I gasp. Just ahead of us sits the burned ruins of what looks to have once been a huge, white stucco building. Broken bricks and twisted rebar litter the ground. I ask what happened here.

"The fire," Lucas says somberly.

During my time on the mountain, I learned that Lama had gone through several periods of disagreement and strife. None was so drastic, however, as the 1996 Hondo Fire, which swept through eight thousand acres of Carson National Forest and destroyed nearly everything at the Lama Foundation. Only two buildings—the Dome one of them—and two cats were left when the evacuated residents returned to the mountain.

"It would have been so easy for people to give up and walk away from all of this," one Lama Bean said about the aftermath of the fire. But the residents were determined to rebuild. "There are a lot of people who love this place very much and worked very hard to make it come back to life," another longtime friend of Lama told me. One friend of Lama planted oak trees to help the forest regrow. When asked how many trees he thinks he planted, he always says, "I stopped counting at ten thousand."

It's 7 A.M. I've been at Lama for about a week. From the distance of my dreams, I hear the soft melody of bells telling me it's time to get out of bed. I don't want to. My sleeping bag is warm and the pile of clothes next to my head smells faintly of lavender soap. But I know I'll be late if I don't get up. Fine.

As soon as I unzip my tent, desert sage and earthy soil embrace my nose. I groggily shake off the remnants of sleep and slowly amble up the dirt path, forgetting about the rock that juts out of the side of the hill, and stub my toe. I fight the urge to yell something obscene, and continue toward the Prayer room. It's time to meditate.

People shuffle over from every direction. Some clutch cups of coffee or jars of tea. Others hug brightly patterned blankets. No one speaks. The community practices silence until breakfast. I approach the tiny, circular hobbit-hole of a door. A hand-painted sign hangs on the handle: *Come with*

Peace. A tiny, high-pitched bell rings to start the meditation. The sound hangs in the air for a minute, and then all goes silent. A half hour slips quietly by, and the tiny bell rings again.

Later in the morning, after breakfast, everyone heads over to the Dome for our morning community meeting— Practice and Tuning. Everyone grabs a pillow and sits in a circle on the floor around the room. Once we are settled in, each person in the circle shares briefly about how they are feeling that morning—"heart tunings." After each person has spoken, someone rings another small bell. It's time for "practical tunings." We're about to learn what chores we're signed up for today. Megan, our chore coordinator—"seva guardian"—reads the list in her slow, relaxed voice. She gets to my name and says I will be responsible for cleaning the Dome.

My shoulders sag as I look around the big, suddenly imposing dome. The floor begins to stretch into an endless, barren plane. So much to clean, *to mop.*

The Ivy League university that had funded my excursion to this place had taught me that sustainability stemmed from the newest technology, world-changing policy, or the biggest research projects. I had spent months fantasizing about the projects I would implement at Lama and the ways I would get to use what I had learned about sustainability in a real-world context. The school could not have designed a person more ready to spread the gospel of academic sustainability than me.

Instead this: daily chores. On my second day I was told

that my primary activities for the next three months would be to clean living spaces and to cook meals for guests and residents. No tinkering with solar panels, no high-level sustainability planning. Just sweeping, chopping, scrubbing . . . mopping. Every day.

This is not what I signed up for.

Megan snaps me out of my horrified daydream when she asks us to stand and hold hands.

"May we serve our community today with love and grace." She looks around the room, beaming.

The meeting disperses, and I wander slowly back toward the kitchen. I stub my toe on another rock; this time I curse out loud. I grab cleaning supplies from the cabinet and trudge back down to the Dome. I glare at the mop and bucket.

With a sigh of resignation, I dip the raggedy mop into the lavender-scented water. My mind wanders to my grad-school friends who were doing exciting research in foreign countries, working for high-level government organizations, and assisting on important policy and technology projects. I sigh, grimacing at my slow progress.

Why didn't I get a nice job at some important government office? Why aren't I in some exotic country doing groundbreaking research? Why am I here, doing this?

I start to hum, and I realize it's a song we sang at our Shabbat service yesterday. I think about the Dome full of people singing and dancing, welcoming a new week. As I replay the night in my mind, I notice the mop running over floors that are already wet. I'm finished. That wasn't so bad.

During dinner that evening, Megan touches me on the shoulder. "Thanks so much for cleaning the Dome, Emily. It looks great!" I look at her for a moment, a look of confusion contorting my face. The sincere gratitude comes as a shock, but I smile back and tell her it was no problem.

After a few weeks, I've settled fairly well into the daily schedule and I decide to try and learn more about what makes Lama the sustainable community it claims to be. I finally ask Sebastian about the solar panels I had seen on my first night on the mountain.

"Those? They're not hooked up to anything. Those panels were a donation, and we're not even sure they work," he says. "We heat our water with propane." I'm baffled. In a place like New Mexico where the sun always shines, solar anything seems like the obvious choice.

I asked another Lama resident, Randy, about the sustainability efforts at Lama. He told me that when he first arrived at Lama, his expectations were high. "I thought more systems were in place—the ideal, perfect systems," he tells me. "But the longer I'm here, the more I realize how haphazard a lot of those systems are." It isn't that these things aren't important to the folks at Lama—they are. The electricity comes from (working) solar photovoltaic panels perched on a south-facing hill. They reduce, reuse, and recycle all they can. But Randy admits that these things just aren't at the top of the priority list. "People call the outhouse a composting toilet, but it's just a damn hole in the ground."

Each conversation leaves me more and more disappointed. What gave this place the right to call itself sustainable? In academia, the key to "greening" almost anything is almost always some kind of technology or policy. Install this or that machine, mandate a different kind of fuel, create a different kind of fuel. That was not what Lama was doing. So what *were* they doing?

Another cool, sage-scented morning. The sky is washed gray with smoke from a nearby forest fire and with storm clouds that refuse to drop rain onto the dusty ground. There hasn't been rain—or any kind of precipitation—up here in months. And you can tell: the flowers that line the walking paths droop with a kind of dry sadness; I can almost hear the creaking aspen trees beg for a drink as I walk by.

I'm on my way to the Spring House for a "water ceremony." Lama gets all of its water from a natural spring that bubbles up to the surface from groundwater fed by meltwater from the mountains. To protect their one source of water from animals or other kinds of contamination, some of the first Lama residents built a small stone house over the spring. Usually, there is more than enough water, and it spills out over its rocky enclosure, but these days, the streambed is dry and cracked; the water is two feet below its normal level.

After our daily reminder to limit ourselves to two five-minute showers per week, we were told that Seth, the farm guru at Lama, would be leading the "water ceremony" later this morning. I was curious to see what that could possibly mean, so I made the trek up to investigate.

When I arrive, Seth is crouching in front of the spring,

head bowed in prayer. Lama Beans wander down in groups of twos and threes and make a semicircle around Seth and the Spring House.

Is this going to be some kind of rain dance?

Seth stretches his arm into the spring to fill a cup with water. He stares into the cup for a moment, takes a sip, and smiles. "None of us would be here without this spring. It's provided so much for us for so long. I just want to invite you all to appreciate the water however you'd like—touch it, sip it, look at it."

As the cup gets passed, most people stare into the cup, touch the water, and then take a sip. A couple of people say a couple of words, but mostly the circle is quiet. When the cup comes to me, I mimic those before me. The water reflects the gray sky and green aspen leaves. When I touch it, I'm shocked by how cold it feels. I take a sip. It tastes a little bit sweet. I've never had water that hasn't passed through some kind of filtration system, and I'm surprised it doesn't taste more like mud or algae. Without thinking, I utter a "thank you" into the cup, and then pass it along.

And then it hits me: no one is asking for more water here.

Everyone is simply thanking the spring, the mountain, the earth, for what water we do have. We aren't doing some kind of weird rain dance hoping the unrelenting gray clouds will finally drop some moisture. We aren't coaxing the gods to give us something. We are just saying thank you, and I wonder why I had never said thank you for water before. It seemed so simple, so straightforward. I mean, I *did* owe my life to the stuff.

Thinking back on the water ceremony, I often wonder what my friends back in academia would have done about a mountain community's water shortage. I imagine a team of scientists would come to test water quality, map the watershed, and monitor flow rates to and from the Spring House. A team of anthropologists would interview the Lama Beans about the water shortage, collect an oral history of water usage in the area, and discuss the meaning of water shortages in other cultures. Someone would organize some kind of conference, where everyone would present their research on this water shortage, discuss possible solutions, and then go home, excited about the "progress" they'd made. Indeed, my friends in academia would know almost everything there is to know about the water that wasn't there as well as the physical and chemical properties of the water that was. Ultimately, the water would be at the center of a problem.

But during the water ceremony, the feeling is jovial. The work my academic peers would do is not worthless. Indeed, if ever there were a severe problem with any part of the landscape, they would be the ones to find a solution. The Lama Beans, however, do whatever they can to prevent such a problem. They make sure every drop is appreciated so that it doesn't go to waste. Even in the driest years, they are able to get by.

It's 7 A.M. I've been at Lama for two months. The wake-up bells are ringing. I've finally gotten used to waking up early. My feet carry me quickly up the path, navigating around the protruding rocks with ease. The routine has become automatic: Bells. Meditate. Bells. Breakfast. Bells. Practice and Tuning. Tiny bell. Heart tunings.

I smile as I listen to what each person has to say. The more I have gotten to know each of the people in the room, the more I've become excited to hear their daily updates. After everyone has spoken, another bell rings, the mood shifts, and we know it's time to hear practical tunings. Megan consults her list; once again, I will be cleaning the Dome.

Megan asks everyone to stand and hold hands. "Today, may we set the intention to serve with love and joy."

Mopping this room with joy? I'll try my best, Megan. But no promises.

I begin to repeat a sort of mantra as I gather my cleaning supplies: It's not so bad. It's not so bad. It's not so bad. When I reenter the Dome, yellow sunlight is pouring through the star-shaped skylight. It's not so bad.

I dip the mop in the lavender water, and begin the slow dance around the room, repeating my mantra with each push of the mop. As I make my way around the room, the words in my head fade away, and I become absorbed in the silence pressing into my ears. My breathing slows to match the rhythm of my movements. And the mop glides leisurely across the wood floor.

I pause to brush the hair out of my face. Sunlight from above makes the freshly mopped floor sparkle like dew on grass early in the morning.

What was I doing here? Cleaning a floor? Was that all? I ran through memory after memory of the many people who walked across these floors. And here I was, not cleaning up after them, but renewing the space for the next set of memories to be made. In the light of a new dawn, the dew shines and reminds us that the day is fresh and ready to be filled with life. Or something like that.

I shake my head out of my musings, dip the mop, and finish mopping the last dry patch of floor.

As the mop runs over the wood, I am struck by how clear the contrast within the wood grains becomes. These aren't just worn-out, dried-out pieces of wood, are they? I imagine the towering trees this floor used to be, and think about the way of honoring the lives of those trees with the efforts I am putting into maintaining them. With each effort of my arms and back, with each slow, rhythmic breath I take, I am giving life back to this space. When people come into this Dome tomorrow, they won't just have a clean floor. The space will be renewed, revitalized, and ready to hold the community again.

I hear the bells signaling that lunch is ready. I pack up my cleaning supplies and head back to the kitchen, where I run into Megan. She touches me on the shoulder and tells me how great it is for me to be there. Then she thanks me for cleaning up the Dome. I smile back. "It was my pleasure."

Even just the small gesture of thanking each other makes the chores at Lama seem better. But it goes deeper than that. Lama isn't just a place where people are more polite. It's a place where a mundane chore like mopping is given value. In mopping a floor, I'm not just the person making the floor clean. I am giving something tangible back to the community of which I am part. And maybe this is what Megan means when she tells us to "serve with love" every morning. Maybe what she means is to serve and *be served* with love. To know that what others do to make the community run smoothly requires each of our actions to have some value beyond their utility.

But how does society make mopping more than just cleaning a floor?

At Lama, part of the answer seems to come from the fact that my coworkers are more than just my neighbors. With every heart tuning, with every hug, the Lama Beans have become people I genuinely love. So appreciating them for what they contribute to our lives together comes easily.

But it's even more than just simple appreciation. Through genuine care for one another and for the land, the Lama Beans are creating a community from the inside out. Life at Lama led to fulfilling relationships with other people, with the land, and with the divine. These relationships drive the desire for a continued existence there.

In academia, my classmates and I are trained to create sustainable communities from the outside. We conduct research, create management plans, and implement the technologies and policies necessary to carry out those management plans. We figure out what the major barriers to implementation will be and then work to remove those barriers. In short, the work is about how best to make the *technology* work, rather than how best to make *our communities* work.

The technology I had once equated with sustainability

is of secondary concern to the Lama Beans. Efforts to do things like replace propane water heaters with solar are sporadic efforts—"when we have time," "when we have money." But efforts to build relationships with one another and with the land are the base of everything they do there.

Lama sustains despite the fact that they have not pursued the newest and most revolutionary technologies, nor have they done extensive research. But they have created a place where it seems like the greatest possible tragedy would be the end of that place. And because of that, the Lama Beans are willing to do what it takes to keep Lama going. It's the only way they ever rebounded from the horror of the Hondo Fire. The Lama Beans are not asking for more water, as I learned at the water ceremony, and really, they're not asking for very much more of anything, except perhaps love and acceptance from their community members.

But even when I was convinced Lama's nonacademic approach to sustainability was an effective one, I was left with this question: What happens when not asking for much becomes the problem itself? What if the water from the spring stops being enough? Can this community really continue using propane to heat its water during the long, hot New Mexico summers? While academia certainly has something to learn from the Lama Bean approach to sustainability, perhaps the Lama Beans have something to learn from academia, too. Rainwater catchment systems, solar heating that works, real composting toilets: all of these are technologies that my academic peers can—and do—help people to adapt in communities around the world.

Trying to force such technologies on a community that may not want them might never work. And the determination of a place like Lama to focus on relationships rather than technology might prevent them from arriving at solutions like those on their own. But academic technical know-how paired with Lama's willpower to sustain might make for the perfect combination.

True to Our Nature

Danna Joy Staaf

Dear offspring,

One of you is two years old; the other is still whiling away
the months in my womb. I'm not expecting either of you
to read this letter for years. But I want to write it now,
while I'm in the midst of spawning.

You will know long before reading it, because your
mother is a biologist, that reproduction is one of the most
mundane acts on the planet. As the lady sang: birds do it,
bees do it, even educated fleas do it. But its universality
also makes it a wondrous, transformative experience.
When I gave birth, I became one of the billions of parents
on our planet, contributing to the endless drama of
creation.

The flip side of life's generative impulse is, of course,
wanton destruction.

By the time you're old enough to read this, you've probably ingested some media suggesting that "nature" is always growing, regenerating, nurturing, and any destruction is caused by "unnatural" humans. For me, it was *FernGully*; for the intermediate generation, it was *Avatar*; for you, probably the same story with new names.

Now, I won't deny that humans have done tremendous environmental damage in the name of "progress"—cutting down forests, polluting the air, extinguishing species. Our destructive skills are currently driving a mass extinction that could be as terrible as the one that ended the dinosaurs' reign. From one perspective, all this violence is unnatural.

From another, it's the most natural thing there could be.

As I write, I'm wearing my favorite maternity shirt, the one a friend so improbably found for sale on the Internet, with a picture of an eight-tentacled robot right over my belly. Everyone assumes we had the shirt custom-made, because of your dad's robotics habit and my decades-long obsession with octopuses. As you're no doubt tired of hearing by now, my first crush was a giant Pacific octopus at the Monterey Bay Aquarium; we met when I was ten and spent two hours with our eyes locked. The creature was alien to me in almost every way (no bones, magic skin, suction cups) and yet so familiar (big eyes, soft breaths, dance moves) I could love her as instantly as any puppy. I'm sure she didn't care about me, because I never fed her—but I never forgot her.

I didn't fall in love with octopuses because they're likely

to survive rampant human depredation of the oceans, but it turns out to be a nice perk. They're such resilient creatures that even though humans have been eating them for as long as we've lived near the ocean, we've never driven a single species extinct.

I'm sorry to tell you that many, many, many other animals are not so lucky.

I wish I could take you to visit the huge flightless moa birds in New Zealand, or the even more enormous sea cows that once swam placidly off our own California coast. Apparently they were too delicious to survive contact with humans. But as long as we're wishing, I also wish we could see ammonites, the massive octopus ancestors with intricately coiled shells that dominated the seas long before fish evolved.

Compared to modern human-caused extinctions, the loss of the ammonites is less tragic for being less immediate. But was it any more natural? We don't know what caused all the extinctions of ancient times, but surely some of yester-millennium's species could have been eaten to death. That's the way of the world. We humans are just far better at it than anyone else.

Unlike the rest of creation, however, we have the urge to overcome our violent side. We can't assign moral rectitude to an asteroid's impact, a virus's devastation, or a shark's rampage. But we ourselves are fiercely moral agents, agonizing over the rightness or wrongness of every decision. I think our morality, rather than our violence, might be our real break from nature.

The ideal of nonviolence runs deep in humanity. Ahimsa, the ancient Sanskrit word for it, was brought to the attention of the Western world by Mahatma Gandhi, but it was hardly a foreign concept. The Ten Commandments say, "Thou shalt not kill," and the Hippocratic oath, "Do no harm."

This moral urge often places us in moral conundrums. For example, you two are second-generation vegetarians. When I was growing up, I was the only one in school, so I fielded a lot of questions. It's going to be easier for you, but if anyone does ask about it, you can give the same answer I always did: We love animals, so we don't eat them. That seems straightforward, right?

Unfortunately, it isn't. As an adult, I get to wonder about things like this: If I order a vegetarian dish at a restaurant that also serves carnivores, am I betraying my principles because my money will help buy meat? Or does my purchase inform the restaurant that vegetarian dishes are popular, thereby prompting the chef to tilt the menu in that direction?

One of you (the one who can already talk) told me recently, "Mama cows make moo milk for baby cows." Hearing this information parroted so earnestly made my hormone-softened heart bleed for the calves whose milk I buy by the gallon. We have friends who are vegan— one is even a pediatrician—and I begin to wonder if that is a better road. On the other hand, we also have friends who make a compelling argument for their ability to encourage humane practices by buying and eating humanely raised and slaughtered meat. They love animals, too.

And there's the question of meat from animals that have already been killed for other reasons. If a wild pig were about to savage one of you and I had the means to shoot it, you bet I would. Then we'd have a pile of pork precursor on our hands, and why not eat it? That situation may seem far-fetched, but it echoes a very real dilemma we face on the continental scale: Millions of introduced pigs threaten the health of the entire North American ecosystem. Do we shoot and eat them? Some vegetarians who won't touch store-bought bacon will dine happily on invasive boar.

The freedom to make moral choices about what we eat is itself a privilege, one that many people around the world don't share. Just as I'd kill an attacking pig to save your lives, I'd also kill a quiet, minding-its-own-business pig to feed you if you were starving. I might cry, but I'd do it. And what if there were no pigs nearby—would I cut down a rain forest to plant a farm? In many places around the world, where "progress" has left in its wake human poverty as well as ecological devastation, people see no option for survival except further damage to the environment.

Africa's island nation of Madagascar could serve as a poster child for such all-inclusive human and environmental suffering. When your dad and I traveled there a few years ago, the flight attendants handed out what I thought of as the Welcome Booklet of Despair. The text detailed in careful French and English the ongoing destruction of the island's stunning biological heritage.

Isolated from all other land for eighty million years, Madagascar evolved a fantastic, almost alien, array of plants, animals, and ecosystems. But in the two thousand years since it was settled by humans, the island's story has gone from breathtaking to heartbreaking: its rain forests burned, its reefs bleached, its lemurs eaten. During the years of isolation, these strange and beautiful primates diversified into remarkable shapes: the minuscule mouse lemur, the singing indri, the tentacle-fingered aye-aye. Now most of about a hundred species are endangered or threatened, primarily by deforestation and hunting. Trees and lemurs are both protected by law, but many impoverished residents can find no work other than logging and poaching.

That's all miserably depressing, but our trip did have a bright spot. We visited some friends working with an outfit called Blue Ventures that tries to address conservation and poverty at the same time. Our friends' particular project helped a group of coastal fishing villages, whose major source of income is octopuses, to set up a marine management system and create reserves to prevent local extinction. So far, it appears remarkably successful. But success, of course, means that octopuses are still being killed—in a careful way that will allow the population to sustain itself. I walked in shallow water one windy morning and watched the fisherwomen stab soft bodies, flip them inside out, and hang them from their fingers.

You two are probably horrified to think of me witnessing that. You've been steeped in my love of octopuses since birth—octopus onesies, octopus toys, octopus books, and octopus posters. "Octopus" was one of the first signs you learned, before you could even talk (the one of you who can talk). Needless to say, I've never eaten octopus.

And yet. I donated happily to Blue Ventures, wanting to support their support of these hardworking women, most of them mothers or grandmothers, catching octopuses to sustain their children and their villages. For many people, in Madagascar and around the world, killing is the only way to make a living.

Although many of our technological advances have risen from the ashes of slashing, burning, and strip-mining— damaging human lives along with the rest of nature—they nevertheless constitute real progress. Progress without quotation marks, progress that I'm glad to leave to you as your birthright. Industrialized agriculture feeds millions; modern medicine has saved at least as many lives, let alone modern plumbing.

And one of my favorite things about modern technology is using it to learn and discover more about nature.

It's true we don't have moas or sea cows anymore, and our world is poorer for it. But at the same time, nature's remaining wonders are open to a much broader audience than they once were. There was a time not too long ago when people like us, born and raised in what is now called California, would know only condors and coyotes. But because of jet engines, I've been able to witness a few of Madagascar's remaining lemurs. You two may see species that I didn't even know existed. Maybe you'll discover them yourselves.

Exploring, building, inventing—these are intrinsic to our humanity, as intrinsic as our desire, not always realized, for nonviolence. What progress we have made, and what damage we have done, both are part of the world now. No matter how much effort we expend, some species that were clinging to existence in my lifetime will disappear in yours. When it comes to octopuses, I expect you could still see any species you like, but that may not be the case if you're unlucky enough to fall in love with lemurs.

"The world is inconveniently arranged for a literal practice of ahimsa," said a Hindu swami named Yukteswar. Challenges range from the trivial (Is it okay to smack that mosquito as long as I feel compassion in my heart?) to the social, economic, and political (Can we forbid people to kill lemurs without helping them find another way to eat and live?).

The world is full of trade-offs. Villager versus octopus. Pig versus the North American ecosystem. Perhaps true ahimsa lies in finding a balance between moving forward and preserving the past, between creation and destruction.

The challenge for us humans isn't how to accomplish

things—it's how to choose the right thing to accomplish. We have the freedom to be carnivores or herbivores, to kill invasives or allow them to kill, to focus on human or nonhuman welfare. The answers usually seem to lie somewhere in the messy, difficult middle.

And remember, you two are the hybrid products of a biologist and an engineer. Not to set up unrealistic expectations, but if anyone can figure this out . . .

Love,
Mom

Acknowledgments

Anthologies, perhaps more than other books, represent the work of communities. At the heart of our community are our contributors, including every young writer who responded to our original call for work. As essays, poems, and stories trickled and then poured in, our admiration grew for the authors' insights, bold experience, convictions, and raw talent. Whether or not a piece appears in the final volume, it helped shape our thinking about our Earth and society at a turning point. All are part of this book and of a vital community conversation that will continue to expand and deepen.

Our many gifted contributors could not have found us without the project's earliest supporters: writers, professors, editors, and readers, who share our belief that young adults' responses to agglomerating environmental crises deserve to be—need to be—heard. H. Emerson Blake, Patrick Carolan, and Stephen Kellert gave valuable advice as we developed our initial proposal, and Ben Goldfarb, Geoff Giller, and David Gonzalez of the Yale School of Forestry and Environmental Studies *Sage Magazine* helped identify potential contributors from their annual Young Environmental Writers Contest. Several colleagues were especially active in helping to solicit contributions from colleges, universities, and other writing programs: Michael Branch, Lisa Couturier, Jeffrey Cramer, Janine DeBaise, Alison Hawthorne Deming, Rue Mapp, Curt Meine, Danyelle O'Hara, Lia Purpura, Rick Van Noy, Terre Ryan, Diana Saverin, Lauret Savoy, and Joseph Spece. Because our call for contributions was passed from one to another, we do not know everyone who generously helped to spread the word, but we greatly appreciate their efforts. Many thanks to one and all.

Other debts of gratitude accumulated over the course of the project. Bill McKibben deserves special thanks for two books that helped inspire this project, *The End of Nature* and *Eaarth*, and for tangible forms of encouragement along the way. Mary Braun, Gregory McNamee, and Ned Tillman gave astute advice on publishing practicalities at key junctures. Steven Pavlos Holmes shared wisdom gained from editing his powerful anthology, *Facing the Change: Personal Encounters with Global Warming*. A stimulating venue to discuss the collection with colleagues and writing students was thoughtfully provided by Ian Marshall. Susan Thornton Hobby lent her keen ear for language and her blithe spirit, and Anna Farb shared valued insights from her perspective as a genuine millennial. Marianne Pettis graciously listened to concerns and questions during much-needed walks around Centennial Lake, and Chiara D'Amore discussed millennial-related social research and lured Julie outside to forget the whole thing occasionally. Three treasured writer friends, Marybeth Lorbiecki, Paula Novash, and Gail Parker, contributed in innumerable ways, from debating grammatical minutiae to lifting their glasses when the book contract was signed.

Our loving husbands, Michael Vogel and Jeff Passe, have also contributed their time, energy, technological savvy, and, especially, patience during the long process of developing, collecting, and preparing this collection for publication.

We are extremely fortunate to work on the anthology with an exceptional editing team at Trinity University Press. From our first encounter, Barbara Ras was warmly encouraging of a still evolving idea. Steffanie Mortis piloted the work through the rough shoals of permissions and peer reviews, always with skill, fortitude, and good humor. Sarah Nawrocki and Burgin Streetman at Trinity, our copy editor Emily Jerman Schuster, and two anonymous peer reviewers are also much admired and appreciated members of the "Coming of Age" community.

The book is dedicated to the millennials we know best—our children and their partners, born in the waning years of the twentieth century: Eli, Hannah, Nathan, and Sarah Vogel, and Jamie Gullen; Jake, Anna, and Parker Rosen; Sara Rosen and Kristiana Kopp; and Ryan and Sarah Passe.

To them, to our esteemed contributors, and to all young adults who have been buffeted by shifts and shocks at the end of nature, we offer love, deep thanks, and a fervent wish for a joyful, venturesome future, on a planet robust and healing.

Credits

"An Orange County Almanac" is adapted from *An Orange County Almanac and Other Essays*, edited by Joseph Zammit-Lucia. Wolf Foundation, 2013. Copyright © Jason Brown. Used with permission of the author.

"The Lives of Plovers" first appeared in *Sage Magazine*. Copyright © Sierra Dickey. Used with permission of the author.

"Rebuild or Retreat" first appeared in *OnEarth*. Copyright © Ben Goldfarb. Used with permission of the author.

"Why I Wear Jordans in the Great Outdoors: A Natural Leader Builds Bridges between Worlds" is reprinted with permission of the Children & Nature Network, childrenandnature.org. Copyright © CJ Goulding.

"The Wager for Rain" first appeared in *Sage Magazine*. Copyright © Megan Kimble. Used with permission of the author.

"Sunset at Mile 16" first appeared in *Sage Magazine*. Copyright © Alycia Parnell. Used with permission of the author.

"Could Mopping Save the World? How Day-to-Day Chores Can Bring Big Changes" first appeared in *Sage Magazine*. Copyright © Emily Schosid. Used with permission of the author.

"Erosion/Accretion" first appeared as "Hydraulic Action" in *Harpur Palate* 13.1. Copyright © Amelia Urry. Used with permission of the author.

Biographies

EDITORS

JULIE DUNLAP has written numerous essays, articles, and children's books about environmental history and the natural world. She is the coeditor, with Stephen R. Kellert, of *Companions in Wonder: Children and Adults Exploring Nature Together.* Her children's books include *Janey Monarch Seed* (forthcoming), *Parks for the People: The Life of Frederick Law Olmsted,* and, with Marybeth Lorbiecki, *Stickeen: An Icy Adventure with a No-Good Dog.* She has examined human relationships with nature since her doctoral studies at Yale University and was a 2016 scholar-in-residence at Grey Towers National Historic Site. She serves on the boards of the Audubon Society of Central Maryland and the Community Ecology Institute and lives with her family in Maryland.

SUSAN A. COHEN is a professor of English and the coordinator of creative writing at Anne Arundel Community

College. She is the editor of *Shorewords: A Collection of American Women's Coastal Writings* and the coeditor, with Florence Caplow, of *Wildbranch: An Anthology of Nature, Environmental, and Place-based Writing*. She has written essays on American literature and the environment, personal essays about place, poetry exploring the legacy of diethylstilbestrol, and poems inspired by people she meets on her daily walks. She won second place in the Dan's Papers Literary Prize for Nonfiction contest, and her poem "She Regards the Polluted Body" was nominated for a Pushcart Prize. An environmental activist, she is a founding board member of the Anne Arundel Patapsco River Alliance, an Anne Arundel Watershed steward, and a Maryland Environmental Trust Land steward.

FOREWORD

BILL MCKIBBEN is a writer and environmentalist who in 2014 was awarded the Right Livelihood Prize, sometimes called the "alternative Nobel." He is the author of more than a dozen books, including *The End of Nature* (1989), regarded as the first work for a general audience about climate change. He is also a founder of 350.org, the first planet-wide, grassroots climate change movement; the Schumann Distinguished Scholar in Environmental Studies at Middlebury College; and a fellow of the American Academy of Arts and Sciences. His honors include the Gandhi Prize, the Thomas Merton Prize, and honorary degrees from eighteen colleges and universities.

CONTRIBUTORS

BLAIR BRAVERMAN's nonfiction has appeared in *This American Life, Orion, The Atavist*, and elsewhere. She is the author of *Welcome to the Goddamn Ice Cube*. She trains and races sled dogs in northern Wisconsin.

JASON M. BROWN is a doctoral candidate at the University of British Columbia. He studied forestry and theology at the Yale School of Forestry and Environmental Studies and Yale Divinity School.

CAMERON CONAWAY is the author of five books, including *Malaria, Poems* (named an NPR Best Book of 2014), and *Chittagong*. His work has appeared in the *Harvard Business Review, Stanford Social Innovation Review*, and *Newsweek*. He is the recipient of the 2015 Daniel Pearl Investigative Journalism Fellowship, and his work has been supported by the Pulitzer Center on Crisis Reporting and the International Reporting Project.

ELIZABETH COOKE, a Wisconsin native, holds degrees from Furman University and Indiana University. After graduation from Furman, she spent a year working on a reforestation project in Gonaïves, Haiti. Cooke now works as a freelance writer, penning technical and creative copy for a variety of publications.

AMY COPLEN is a doctoral student at Portland State University, where her work focuses on the intimate connection between the exploitation of people and nature, and the efforts of activists, workers, and consumers to create just and sustainable cities. Coplen holds undergraduate degrees from the University of New Mexico and a master's degree from Yale University.

BEN CROMWELL lives in Salt Lake City with his wife and two children. He is the author of *Touch: Making Contact with Climate Change*, and his work has appeared in *Sage Magazine, Flyway*, and *High Desert Journal*. He is the program director for Playworks Utah.

SIERRA DICKEY is a native of Cape Cod, Massachusetts, with additional roots in Vermont. She holds an undergraduate degree from Whitman College, where her honors thesis received the Linda Meyer Award for Best Environmental Essay.

BEN GOLDFARB is a correspondent at *High Country News*. His writing has appeared in *OnEarth, Scientific American, Hakai Magazine*, and *Earth Island Journal*. He has a master's degree from the Yale School of Forestry and Environmental Studies, where he served as editor-in-chief of *Sage Magazine*.

CJ GOULDING is the lead organizer for the Natural Leaders Network. He has worked with the Youth Programs Office of the National Park Service and as a community crew leader for high school students in city parks and has led backcountry backpacking and canoe trips for high school students. He is working on his master's degree in education at Antioch University in Seattle.

BONNIE FRYE HEMPHILL, a North Carolina native and sometime Vermonter, Mainer, and Seattleite, wrote her essay as a graduate student at the Yale School of Forestry and Environmental Studies. She continues to accelerate clean energy economic development in all corners of the United States.

LISA HUPP is a ten-year resident of Kodiak Island, Alaska, where she works as a park ranger for the Kodiak National Wildlife Refuge and as an adjunct instructor at the University of Alaska, Anchorage. Her work has appeared in *Orion*, *Refuge Update*, and *Fish and Wildlife News*.

AMARIS KETCHAM is an honorary Kentucky Colonel who teaches graphic design and print production in the University of New Mexico Honors College. Her work has recently appeared in *Eleven Eleven*, the *Los Angeles Review*, the *Rumpus*, and the *Utne Reader*.

MEGAN KIMBLE lives in Tucson, Arizona, where she is the managing editor of *Edible Baja Arizona*, a food magazine serving Tucson and the borderlands. She is the author of *Unprocessed: My City-Dwelling Year of Reclaiming Real Food* and a regular contributor to the *Los Angeles Times*.

CRAIG A. MAIER lives among the kettle ponds, glacial hills, and rocky ridges of south-central Wisconsin. His work has appeared in *American Forests* and *Boatman's Quarterly Review*, and he has served as editor and contributor to the *Leopold Outlook*, the Aldo Leopold Foundation's member magazine.

ABBY MCBRIDE, a self-described sketch biologist, makes art and writes stories exploring nature, evolution, and ecology. She has degrees from Williams College and the Massachusetts Institute of Technology and professional experience as a bird researcher, lobster boat helmsman, pianist, and pastry chef.

LAUREN MCCRADY was born and raised in Oregon's Willamette Valley. As an undergraduate at Westminster College in Salt Lake City, she cultivated a love for the Colorado Plateau. After finishing graduate work at the University of Nevada, she moved to Moab, Utah, where she teaches high school English.

JAMES ORBESEN is a professor from Chicago and author of *Gud Dog: Examining Grant Morrison and Frank Quietly's We3* (forthcoming from Sequart). His work has appeared in the *Atlantic, Salon, Jacobin, Guernica,* and *PopMatters.*

ALYCIA PARNELL holds a degree in environmental studies from the University of Utah and lives, works, and writes in Salt Lake City. Her work has appeared in *Sage Magazine* and *Scribendi.*

EMILY SCHOSID is a sustainability planner at Virginia Tech. She holds a master's degree from the Yale School of Forestry and Environmental Studies. Her poetry has appeared in a variety of literary journals around Colorado and the Internet.

DANNA JOY STAAF is a freelance science writer, editor, and novelist. Her first book, about the evolution of modern squid from ancient sea monsters, is forthcoming from the University Press of New England. She lives with her family in California.

WILLIAM THOMAS helped found the intentional community Baltimore Free Farm, an urban farm and social center that became a multi-home housing cooperative, in 2010. He recently struck out into the world on his bike, seeking adventure, treasure, and social justice.

AMELIA URRY, an editor at Grist.org, writes regularly about climate, culture, and change. A science writer and poet, she is writing a book on fractal geometry with mathematician Michael Frame, forthcoming from Yale University Press.